CHRISTIAN
METAPHYSICS

CHRISTIAN
METAPHYSICS

by Claude Tresmontant

translated by Gerard Slevin

Preface by Walter J. Ong, S.J.

SHEED AND WARD – NEW YORK

Christian Metaphysics was first published in French, under the title *Les idées maîtresses de la métaphysiques chrétienne,* by Editions du Seuil, Paris.

Library of Congress Catalog Card Number 65-20866

Nihil Obstat
    Edward J. Montano, S.T.D.
    Censor Librorum
Imprimatur
    Terence J. Cooke,
    Vicar General
New York, N.Y., August 20, 1965
The nihil obstat and imprimatur are official declarations that a book or pamphlet is free of doctrinal or moral error. No implication is contained therein that those who have granted the nihil obstat and imprimatur agree with the contents, opinions or statements expressed.

Manufactured in the United States of America

To Paul-André Lesort

Preface

IT IS STRANGE that we have had no book quite like this
before. We have had works which explain the consonance
between metaphysics and Catholic teaching, others which
consider the metaphysical questions arising in the context
of Christian teaching or living, and still others which argue
one or another of the theories regarding the relationship between metaphysics and theology or between metaphysics
and dogma. Everyone is quite aware that metaphysics and
the Church's teachings are somehow related. Indeed, often
a purportedly "reasoned" metaphysics may be in fact a distil-
lation from Catholic teaching as such rather than from
natural existence in itself. But, so far as I know, no other
book in any language undertakes frankly the basic task of
going openly to the documents of the Catholic faith, that
is, to the Bible and the decrees of the Church councils and
of the popes from the beginning to the present day, with
the avowed aim of stating in summary form the metaphysics
they imply and, indeed, often explicitly state.

This is what M. Claude Tresmontant here undertakes to
do. He employs the term metaphysics in a large and accepted sense, as referring to a first or fundamental philosophy, or perhaps simply to philosophy in its quintessen-

tial state, an understanding of what is most basic in natural existence, a body of truth concerned with "being, the distinction between uncreated and created being, the one and the many, becoming, matter, the temporal, man, the human soul, the corporeal, liberty, thought, action" (in his own words). Concerning such matters he finds in Church documents nothing new to scholars, as he himself makes clear in his opening pages. All the philosophical truths he identifies in Christian teaching have long been known to be there. Nevertheless, because the truths have not been assembled elsewhere in this straightforward form the present book is refreshing and valuable.

As everyone knows, there has been a long and sometimes heated dispute as to whether one can speak of a Christian metaphysics or of a Christian philosophy, any more than one can speak of a Christian mathematics or a Christian chemistry. M. Tresmontant does not undertake to resolve this dispute, but he gives it perspective, largely by highlighting just how different the metaphysics implied by Christian teaching is from anything else in the history of thought. Pointing to the body of truths he has assembled, he observes in effect: (1) all this is to be found, directly or by implication, in what the Church teaches; (2) it is metaphysics and by right accessible to reason; but (3) it is, as a whole, and even in certain of its major parts, not taught by any non-Christians at all so far as we can discover. The present work thus reinforces what others have asserted but have not so directly documented: there is a Christian metaphysics, as there is a Newtonian or an Einsteinian physics. It is Christian not because only Christians can know it but because it was Christians (working with the entire Hebreo-

Christian heritage and under divine grace) who discovered it, although they did not do so alone in the sense that they drew also on non-Hebrew and non-Christian heritages in the process.

The author, to take one example, indicates how the totally fundamental Christian doctrine of the absolute, transcendent, free God as radically, ontologically different from the world which is His creation is in one way or another contrary to Brahmanism, Platonism, Aristotelianism, Neoplatonism, Spinozism, and the later philosophies of German idealism. Or again, Plato and Aristotle taught that the heavenly bodies are suprahuman animated beings: Christianity taught they are no such thing at all. Particularly today, it is valuable to point out, as M. Tresmontant does, how Christian metaphysics is grounded in the Bible itself despite the fact that the ancient Hebrews were not formal philosophers and possessed an articulate metaphysics only by implication. Implication is often powerful and clear.

M. Tresmontant is perhaps best known to English-language readers for his *Pierre Teilhard de Chardin: His Thought*, a pioneer interpretive work which is still one of the most serviceable brief introductions to the French Jesuit's now widely studied writings on the nature and meaning of evolution. Although this present work connects more obviously with other books of M. Tresmontant's (several now also available in English) on the development of Hebrew thought and of early Christian thought, it can readily be related also to his interest in Father Teilhard. Teilhard undertook to relate the development of the natural, secular world to the Catholic faith. M. Tresmontant, too, is here exploring relationships between the natural world of thought and Catholic faith, and doing so in straightforward historical fashion. He is aware of the anthropological and historical structures in abstract thought and he does not propose his present outline of Christian metaphysics as at all a closed system. It is true, and growing as well.

The relationship of the natural world to the Catholic faith is no simple matter: indeed, the relationship itself is part of the mystery of faith, open to gradually enlarged intellectual exploration but never fully interpreted. The Catholic faith is not set off against natural understanding: although it reaches beyond this understanding, it also reaches through it. The faith has always interacted vigorously with human thought as this thought undergoes its natural development. Today the interaction is more energetic than it has been for centuries, perhaps than it has ever been before. We have become more reflectively conscious of the interaction through our vastly deepened understanding of history and of process, and, with Vatican Council II, we have finally undertaken even to program the interaction.

There can be little doubt that the philosophy implied in the Church's teaching is destined for massive and fascinating growth in the years ahead. The facts of evolution have already proved congenial to the Hebreo-Christian tradition at the very points where they are embarrassing to other religious traditions. For the Hebreo-Christian tradition sees time and what happens in time as having a positive value, and as being a direct concern of God Himself, whereas other religions tend to flee from time and its fruits, taking time as somehow evil. For the Christian, God's concern with events in time reaches the point where He actually takes to

Himself a human nature in time, in the Person of Jesus Christ, Himself God. Moreover, present-day interest in the human person, in personality structures and their correlation with man's social evolution, in depth psychology, and in intersubjectivity promise vigorous interaction with Catholic teaching all the way up to the heights of Trinitarian theology, the theology of the three divine Persons. As we look ahead in these and other areas to interactions between growing natural knowledge and the faith, the present book will stand us in good stead. It will enable us to cast up accounts as they stand at present and to take our bearings for the future.

As we look ahead, we are also aware of course that, today more than ever before, thinking in and with the Church is a cosmopolitan activity. It cannot be carried on in any one or two or three isolated linguistic milieux. Works in one language must be made available in others. Hence this translation from the French is most welcome in the English-speaking world. Although our French friends still refer to this world somewhat quaintly as *le monde anglo-saxon*, the present very readable English version is nicely cosmopolitan. Mr. Gerard Slevin is a skilled Irish user of the language and his translation will be of service not only to the "Anglo-Saxons" across the Channel but also to a greater number of native English speakers across the seas whose ancestry varies from Anglo-Saxon to African, Polish, Italian, American Indian, and beyond.

WALTER J. ONG, S.J.

Saint Louis University

Contents

Contents

Introduction

IN AN EARLIER WORK[1] I tried to show how, in the first centuries of our era, Christianity gradually became aware of its own requirements, its own principles, and metaphysical structure. We saw how Christian thought gropingly discovered its own nature, in innumerable controversies, from the metaphysical point of view. I brought this work up to the time of Saint Augustine only, and tackled only those problems which are dealt with in this first, youthful period of Christianity. I could continue to show how in subsequent centuries Christianity became aware of other constituent and properly philosophic requirements.

The work proposed here is different, in its method and in its point of view. I wish to describe in brief outline the structure of Christian metaphysics without taking into consideration its slow evolution or its patient groping towards self-awareness but extracting the properly metaphysical content of solemn definitions which often are binding on the whole Church. Instead of following step by step the discovery by Christian thought of its own needs and its own

1 *La Métaphysique du christianisme et la Naissance de la philosophie chrétienne*, Paris, 1961.

metaphysical principles, I propose to give here a synthetic account from specially decisive texts, garnered more often than not from the Acts of Ecumenical Councils or from pontifical texts. In these texts it is no longer this or that Father or Doctor of the Church who speaks, but indeed the universal Church. Here orthodox Christian thought in its universality is given its expression.

The brief outlines which I offer here aim simply at showing, by describing in bold outline its general structure for the sake of those who deny it, that a Christian metaphysic does exist. It remains to develop later each point in particular, to explore thoroughly in each of the directions indicated here.

The sketches which I offer in the following pages do not therefore seek to constitute more than a programme which is entirely provisional, tentative, and open to later corrections and developments. It is an obviously general working plan rather than a finished work. A synoptic account of this kind can sometimes be of assistance in preparing and placing particular researches. It is also obvious that the present outline, set down for myself, is not addressed to the learned. They will learn nothing here. It is addressed to those who, starting like myself from a complete ignorance of these problems, wish to initiate themselves gradually into the Church's thought from the metaphysical point of view. Starting from this common ignorance I have thought that it was perhaps not entirely useless to communicate, as my own enquiries proceeded, the results of my reading to those who do not have the leisure to engage in such research. The ignorant man who discovers what the learned have known for a long time is sometimes better able to expound more simply, and in language better adapted to the general ignorance, truths which are quite new to his eyes, and which he marvels at savoring for the first time, even though in themselves they are ancient. In mathematics it is sometimes good that elementary truths should be discovered by beginners and expounded to their companions. Perhaps the same hold true in metaphysics and in theology?

Opinions held up to the present with regard to the problem of Christian philosophy divide themselves into many camps. Some assert that such a Christian philosophy does not exist, that the expression itself is meaningless, and that a Christian philosophy does not exist any more than a Christian mathematics or a Christian physics. This is the opinion maintained by Émile Bréhier in his *Histoire de la Philosophie* as well as in several noteworthy articles published in the *Revue de Métaphysique et de Morale* in 1931.

Others, on the contrary, hold that there are not one but many possible Christian philosophies, that Christianity is compatible, compossible, with many philosophies. They claim for the philosopher who is a Christian the liberty to chose or to evolve for himself a philosophy which is not subject to the jurisdiction of theology, in order not to fall into an error analogous to that of wanting to construct a "system of politics drawn from the Old Testament".

The thesis which I submit to the critical examination of the reader is that there is *one* Christian philosophy and one only. I maintain, in other words, that Christianity calls for a metaphysical structure which is not any structure, that

Christianity is an original metaphysic. I maintain that Christian theology and Christian dogma contain in themselves a metaphysical substructure, a body of very precise and very well-defined theses which are properly metaphysical, though it is only progressively with time, in the course of its history, that Christian thought becomes conscious of it.

I have tried to show this elsewhere, starting from Holy Scripture. I have tried to show that Scripture in fact requires, either explicitly or implicitly, a body of theses or doctrines which can only be called metaphysical. They concern being, the distinction between uncreated being and created being, the one and the many, becoming, matter, the temporal, man, the human soul, the corporeal, liberty, thought, action, and so forth. I then tried to show that Christian thought in the first centuries became progressively and even gropingly aware of possessing, of comprising, a group of requirements, principles, doctrines, and theses which are also properly metaphysical and which concern those same points which I have just noted—that is to say, an original doctrine of being, an ontology radically different from that of the Hellenic philosophies, a doctrine of the absolute and a doctrine of sensible being, as also of their relationship; a doctrine of the world, of matter, of becoming, of time; a very precise anthropology which clarified itself by ruling out certain theses incompatible with the very principles of Christianity; a doctrine of action, of liberty, of thought. In those studies already published I have tried to show, by beginning at the beginning (that is to say, from the biblical root of Christian thought), how Christianity involves a very precise metaphysic, how in fact it is an original metaphysic set against existing metaphysics, whether those are of India, Greece, non-Christian, or partly christianized modern Europe.

But I could have proceeded in another way. For over two thousand years, the Church has defined its thought in a certain number of solemn texts formulated by Ecumenical Councils or by Popes. A good many of these texts contain affirmations or assertions which are properly metaphysical and which we may examine separately. Scripture, the consensus of the Fathers and Doctors of the Church, the solemn definitions of Ecumenical Councils and of Popes, all show that Christian thought involves a certain number of very exact metaphysical theses of which it suffices to draw up an inventory. From the Jahwist document, drawn up in writing about the ninth century before our era, up to the canons of the Vatican Council in 1870, an original, metaphysical tradition unfolds, grows, defines itself, and formulates itself.

This group of properly metaphysical theses can be arranged under a certain number of headings, thus forming a systematic account of Christian metaphysics as far as it has, at this moment, become aware of itself. This awareness is certainly not complete any more than we have an explicit and exhaustive awareness of the revelation which is entrusted to the Church.

I have previously tried to show the convergence, among many Christian thinkers, of Christian thought about certain metaphysical theses which revealed themselves as inherent in Christianity itself. It is a collective thought which should

reveal itself, the thought of the Church. As long as one
invokes only the authority of such and such a Christian
thinker, or of such and such a Father or Doctor of the
Church, it is always possible to dispute whether such a
doctrine, taught by a master of Christian thought, is a necessary part of Christianity. Christian thought, the thought
of the Church, has not followed its greatest Doctors in all
their doctrines. It has selected. A single authority does not
therefore suffice to establish that a particular doctrine,
metaphysical or theological, is in fact the thought of the
Church. But on the other hand the convergence, the in-
creasingly unanimous consensus, attests that such is indeed
the thought of the Church, particularly if this consensus is
confirmed by a solemn definition, by an Ecumenical Council. In an Ecumenical Council it is the thought of the
Church which formulates itself and makes itself explicit. If
metaphysical propositions are contained in these solemn
definitions, it will not be possible to dispute that it is indeed
the metaphysics of Christianity, formulated by the whole
Church, which here finds its expression.

While I was applying myself only to bringing out this
convergence of Christian thought about certain metaphysical certitudes by texts from the Fathers, it was possible to
dispute the method. It was possible to put forward the
hypothesis that we had chosen such texts from such Fathers
precisely because they converge. But when a solemn definition of an Ecumenical Council has come to seal this convergence, it is seen that this is the effect of a real curvature
of Christian thought, a real curvature of the universe of
Christian thought in which Christian thinkers apply them-

selves to thinking. If the many texts which I have gathered together in my previous work converge, it is not because I may have chosen them in a systematic and arbitrary manner for the sake of their convergence, brushing aside those which did not suit my purpose. Rather, it is because the Fathers of the Church did not strive to be original or eccentric but on the contrary to think with the Church, *sentire cum Ecclesia*. The convergence of the texts noted shows the curvature of a universe of thought in which the Fathers wish to place themselves. When a doctrine, such as that of Origen, for example, presents itself to us as eccentric and original in comparison with the Christian, philosophic tradition, I have not covered it up or minimized it. On the contrary, I have set forth fully the metaphysical system of the *De Principiis*, emphasizing every incompatibility with Christianity which this system involves. But we have also seen how Christian thought reacted to this system, how it asserted itself, and became more aware of itself in reaction.

The Fathers of the Church do not say "my philosophy", but "our philosophy".

Christian thought therefore presents an original, exceptional phenomenon. A school of philosophy—the Platonic, for example, or the Aristotelian, or the Neoplatonic—presents some constants in the thesis upheld. It displays a tradition of thought, a certain homogeneity. But the authors do not refuse to depart from this tradition, to break with it, to be original. In Christian thought, the authors, the Fathers and Doctors, are uniquely desirous of being faithful to the thought of the Church and of not deviating from it. They do not seek to invent an original system. On the contrary, indeed, the idea is repugnant to them. They seek to think with the tradition. They constantly invoke their predecessors. Above all they call upon Holy Scripture, which is their rule and their criterion. One can say that in the case of these thinkers it is a collective thought which is being elaborated, the thought of a body. The thought of the Church is a reality much more organic and homogeneous than the tradition of thought of any philosophical school whatsoever. The aspiration of the Christian Fathers and Doctors is to be an active cell or an active and creative member of this body which is the Church, in order to make it grow according to the analogy of the rule of faith. One cannot then compare this phenomenon which is orthodox Christian thought with any school of philosophy. It is a unique phenomenon.

At the end of my long exploration in this largely untrodden forest which constitutes the Christian literature of the first centuries of our era, I had arrived at certain conclusions—classic conclusions, moreover. Orthodox Christian thought in the first centuries did not assimilate—did not gulp down, if one may so put it—the contribution of Greek philosophy, as certain historians have affirmed with delight or disapproval. Orthodox Christian thought in the first centuries selected, in Greek philosophy, those elements which appeared to it to be capable of being turned to account, and rejected those metaphysical theses which seemed to it to be incompatible with its own principles and requirements. This is to say that Christian thought rejected the most original and the most constant theses of ancient

metaphysics. We are therefore very far from the pure and
simple invasion of Christianity by Greek philosophy, which
a number of historians thought they discerned. This work
of selection and rejection, carried out by orthodox Christian thought in the first centuries, is described by Leo XIII
in his encyclical devoted to Christian philosophy, *Aeterni
Patris,* of August 4, 1879:

> If now, Venerable Fathers, you examine the history
> of philosophy, you will find there the proof of all that
> we have just said. Indeed among the ancient philoso-
> phers who did not have the benefit of the faith even
> those who were considered the wisest fell, in many
> points, into monstrous errors. You will not be un-
> aware how many false and absurd things they teach,
> along with some truths, how many uncertain and
> doubtful things, touching the nature of the divinity,
> the first origin of things, the government of the world,
> the knowledge which God has of the future, the cause
> and principle of evils, the last end of man and eternal
> bliss, the virtues and vices and other points of doctrine
> of which the true and certain knowledge is absolutely
> necessary for the human race.
>
> On the contrary, the first Fathers and Doctors of
> the Church, understanding very well that in the pur-
> poses of the divine will Christ is the restorer of learn-
> ing because he is the power of the wisdom of God,
> and 'because in him are hidden all the treasures of
> wisdom and knowledge', these Fathers and Doctors
> undertook to search the books of the ancient philoso-

phers and to compare their opinions with revealed
doctrines. By an intelligent choice they adopted what
in those philosophies appeared to conform with the
truth and wisdom, and as for the rest, they rejected
what they were unable to correct. For just as God in
his admirable providence raised up for the defence of
the Church against the curelty of tyrants heroic
martyrs who were nobly unsparing of their lives, so
against the sophists and the heretics he set men of
profound wisdom who might take care to defend,
even by the aid of human reason, the treasure of revealed truths. Even from the birth of the Church,
Catholic doctrine encountered most stubborn adver-
saries, who, holding up to derision Christian dogmas
and principles, affirmed that there were several gods,
that the material world has neither beginning nor
cause, that the course of things is not governed by the
plan of divine Providence, but is moved by some blind
power or other and by an inevitable necessity. Against
these fomenters of senseless doctrines, opportunely
rose up learned men, known as "apologists", who,
guided by the faith, proved by means of arguments,
taken if necessary from human wisdom, that we must
adore one God, endowed in the highest degree with all
kinds of perfection; that by his omnipotence all things
have come out of nothing; that they subsist by his
wisdom, and by it are moved and directed each towards its proper end.

In my former work, devoted to the first centuries, I had to specify that it was the metaphysics of orthodox Christianity, the metaphysics of orthodoxy, which was in question. As a matter of fact, it is evident that the "heresies" of the first centuries obey metaphysical principles, implicit or explicit, which are precisely different from those which can be discovered in orthodox theology. Without coming to a decision (such was not my role) on the merits of the terms "orthodoxy" or "heresy", I chose to study the orthodox *phylum* or stem of thought, bringing to light the differences which exist at the metaphysical level between orthodox Christian thought and the "side-shoots" which separated from it.

In the present sketches I must recall the same methodological distinctions. We are studying here a metaphysic which expresses itself in solemn definitions, occasioned generally, if not always, by controversies, heresies, schisms. We follow therefore a main "stem" which is expressly distinguishable from other "species" or "families" of Christian thought. Without coming to a decision in this case either (this would be matter for another work), I describe the metaphysics of the Catholic "stem" of Christian thought and when we read the properly metaphysical definitions or the definitions with metaphysical content of the Council of Trent and the first Vatican Council, we shall have occasion to remark that at the metaphysical level perceptible differences appear between Catholic theology and the theologies born of the Reformation. Perhaps indeed it is at the metaphysical level that the choices are made which govern the theological divergences.

The sketches which I propose here are based mostly on conciliar definitions. These conciliar definitions do not express the whole thought of the Church. They formulate only what has been questioned, what has been disputed, or deflected. Therefore a margin exists between what is defined by the Church and what, without being defined, is part of the Church's thought. I confine myself here to solemn definitions because they represent and reveal the incontestable formulation of a minimum, which suffices to demonstrate the existence of a Christian metaphysic and to bring out the general structure. But the thought of the Church extends widely beyond that which has been defined. It is then in the broad stream of Christian tradition that we must search for this consensus which expresses, on the metaphysical plane, certitudes connatural with Christian theology. There is material here for many monographs.

The idea itself of Christian metaphysics can give rise to dispute from many points of view. It will very rightly be said that metaphysics is a conceptual technique located at the level of philosophical reflection. There is nothing of the sort in the Old Testament or in the New; there is nothing of the sort in the Christian incunabula. Certainly the Old and New Testaments do not contain books devoted to treating explicitly, technically, academically, problems of being, of becoming, of time, of the sensible, of matter, of the soul, of liberty, of action, of thought, and so forth. But they contain "positions" on these several problems, "attitudes of thought", which are wrapped up in a context which is not technically philosophical, but which are nonetheless aware of themselves. The proof is that biblical thought, and afterwards Christian thought, whether confronted with Assyrio-Babylonian mythologies, or Gnostic myths, or certain philosophical theses, constantly and continuously reject and dismiss doctrines and myths which contain, in a manner equally obscure, positions which are contrary or inverse.

The metaphysic contained in Holy Scripture, as often as not in an implicit and concealed fashion, was not formulated in philosophical treatises. It exists nonetheless. An organism requires an anatomical structure, even though this anatomy has not been described and formulated in an anatomical treatise. Biblical thought, and after it Christian thought, involve an original, metaphysical structure, even before this structure is described and formulated in a technical and explicit fashion.

But there is more. In fact, the metaphysics of Scripture expresses itself occasionally, on fundamental points, in an explicit manner. Thus the biblical doctrine of being is expressed in the very first line of the Bible when the theological school, which biblical criticism terms "sacerdotal", sets forth the fundamental distinction which exists between God and the world, and the creation of the world by God. A double ontology comes to light, that of uncreated being and that of created being. Is this not metaphysics?

In the first centuries of the Christian era the metaphysics inherent in Scripture clarifies itself, formulates itself, and meditates upon itself, thanks to the opposition found to exist between the theses which made up biblical metaphysics and certain theses taken from a Hellenic tradition of thought and a Hellenic culture. It is not, of course, a question of contrasting biblical thought and Christian thought in an over-simplified way with Hellenism as such. That would be to fall into a philosophic form of Manicheism, or rather into a Manicheism transferred to the history of philosophy. It is a simple question of recognizing that Christian thought held itself to be incompatible with certain very precise theses and doctrines taken from Platonism, Aristotelianism, Stoicism, and Neoplatonism.

From the first Christian generations Christian thought formulated for itself its own philosophical theses in a language often borrowed from the Hellenic culture. After encountering philosophical theses which it deemed incompatible with its own requirements, with its own constitutive principles, Christian thought set about technically philosophizing. A Christian philosophy exists from the moment in which Christian thought reflects, technically and rationally, upon the metaphysical conditions of its own content, taken from Scripture.

In connection with this kind of research I have occasionally heard friendly voices mention the word "integrism". In studying the metaphysical structure of biblical thought, the metaphysical content of Christian dogma, the anatomy and physiology, on the metaphysical plane, of the Jewish and Christian stream of thought, I seem to threaten philosophical liberty. I answer that my purpose, up to the present, has been simply descriptive. I have thought to perceive and to be able to describe a metaphysical anatomy in this body— or better, this original species which is Hebraic and Christian thought. The first question is to know whether or not a metaphysical anatomy exists. If I have described no more than a phantom, if what I had thought I saw does not exist, the question is settled. But if indeed Christian thought comprises, on the metaphysical plane, a certain functional anatomy, which is not any sort of anatomy, and which is necessary for the life of the body, then it is not he who attempts to describe it who is to be reproached with the exigencies which any structure involves. Orthodox Christian thought is not compatible, from the metaphysical point of view, with just anything at all, exactly as in a quite different order the anatomical and physiological structures of an organism involve certain laws of existence which are not just any laws. The biologist who describes this anatomical structure and these laws of physiological existence is not taken to task for limiting our freedom.

We must then, it seems, examine in the first place a question of fact.

But if Christian thought, if Christianity involves on the metaphysical plane, as on the theological, certain exigencies of homogeneity and consistency, the analogy of faith, it does not entail any risk for our freedom of thought. For liberty does not consist in being able to choose between several positions, of which some are false and others true, but in finding the truth. Where the Spirit of the Lord is, there is freedom. The amorphous, the indeterminate, and the vague are not more favorable to liberty than structure and organization.

Nevertheless, we readily acknowledge that in metaphysics, as in theology, the analysis of the structures and theses constitutive of Christian thought presents a risk of integrism. Integrism consists essentially in hardening and making concrete that which is *in via*, in development, in genesis. Integrism is a fixation to the letter. Orthodoxy is spirit. But the spirit is not without structure. Integrism consists in makng ill-considered and despotic deductions from theological definitions which often did not have in view the problem for which exploitation of them has been sought. Orthodoxy is life—but life, once again, presupposes and constitutes structures and an organization. It is possible to misuse these structures and this organization of thought, so as to hinder a legitimate and healthy development; that is integrism. But this very real danger must not lead to a failure to recognize the existence of the structure and of the functional and definite organization.

Today Christian philosophy is very far from having become aware of all that it implies, necessitates, comprises in itself, all that it is, just as Catholic theology has not finished becoming aware explicitly of its content, and has not exhausted the deposit of revelation. An order remains, and obscure, indeterminate zones—problems open to the free discussion of theologians and philosophers. The solutions in these immature domains remain free, to the extent that they locate themselves entirely within the analogy of the faith, and are compatible with the whole of the organism of Christian thought. Thus, to keep to the philosophical plane, one may legitimately ask oneself today to what extent idealism is compatible with Christianity. If idealism consists in denying, as Fichte did, the creation of beings and the radical, ontological distinction between the divine ego and the human ego, if idealism identifies itself with pantheism, then certainly idealism is incompatible with Christianity. But if idealism consists simply in denying the existence of a material thing existing outside the mind, while maintaining the real creation of thinking subjects, then one does not see—for the moment at least—any fundamental and essential incompatibilities with Christianity. In place of a monadology of a pantheistic type, in which the thinking substances are eternal sparks and fulgurations born of the divine source and consubstantial with this source of original *focus*, we are dealing with a Christian monadology, in which the objectivity of material substance is regarded as superfluous. It is possible to debate from a philosophical point of view the merits of such a philosophy. One cannot, it seems, accuse it of heresy. All things happen as if material substance comprised an objective existence, independent of the thinking, human mind. This existence, in the idealist hypothesis, is only a representation. Practically, nothing is changed. The discussion remains open on the philosophical plane, and the philosopher will ask himself what, in these conditions, the existence of the universe and of life several milliards of years before man can mean.

By this example I wished to indicate only one of the instances in which Christian philosophy remains undetermined in part and capable of admitting, at least provisionally, solutions equally legitimate. In these freely discussed questions there exists therefore, in fact, a philosophical pluralism. But as Christian thought progresses, it rules out certain doctrines and certain theses as incompatible with its internal exigencies. This is as evident on the theological plane as on the metaphysical. Christian thought progresses thus in apophatic manner, following the *via negativa*. But this proceeding, by which Christian thought rules out that which is incompatible with its principles, the organization of a positive and formed body of thought is possible, even though this may be unfinished and in genesis. The freedom of the Christian philosopher lies in this genesis in which he must co-operate, not in the structure of the knowledge already attained, which indeed imposes on him certain well-defined functional exigencies.

It has sometimes been said that it is just as absurd to claim to extract a metaphysic from the Bible as a system of politics from the Old Testament. Certainly we would not seek political principles in a text of Deuteronomy which recommends the massacre of the enemies of Israel. But at the risk of damaging my case I will admit that, in my view, Christianity is no more compatible with any system of politics whatsoever than it is with any philosophy whatsover. Christianity, at the ethical level—and this level is moreover accessible to the natural reason—comprises principles which govern both politics and individual life. But that is another story.

CHAPTER ONE

The Doctrine
of the Absolute

THE DOCTRINE OF THE ABSOLUTE according to Christianity is original if it is compared with the doctrine of the absolute according to Brahmanism, Platonism, Aristotelianism, Neoplatonism, Spinozism, or the other later philosophies, in particular those of German idealism.

According to Christianity the absolute is not the world, or—what comes to the same thing—the world is not the absolute. The world is not uncreated, eternal, ontologically sufficient. Neither is the world something of the absolute; it is not a shadow of the absolute, nor an emanation, nor a modality of the divine substance. Rather, the world is radically, ontologically other than the absolute. It is not of divine essence nor of divine nature. Nature is not absolute mind alienated, petrified, or exiled.

According to Christianity the absolute is unique. Things could be conceived otherwise; and in fact religions and philosophies have often conceived things differently. According to the Egyptian and Assyrian cosmogonies, for example, primeval chaos is the uncreated and eternal absolute. The divine is born of this primeval chaos. It is not the divine which is, properly speaking, the absolute. According to these religions there is, as in Hesiod, a genealogy of the gods and goddesses and a battle of gods at the beginnings of history. A polytheism which would grant the predicates of the absolute (aseity, eternity, ontological sufficiency, and so forth) to several gods would multiply the absolute. In Manichean dualism we have a case where the predicates of the absolute are attributed to two principles: matter, the evil principle, and the good, the right and luminous principle. We are therefore dealing here with two absolutes. In the cosmology of Aristotle the world is uncreated, eternal, imperishable. It is the absolute. The divine, if it is distinct from it—a question which we shall not examine here— constitutes another absolute. Christianity has rejected at one and the same time both polytheism and Manichean dualism. Christianity professes a single and unique absolute.

According to Christianity the absolute from all eternity is blissful, uncreated, ontologically sufficient, without birth and without becoming, without genesis. Christianity repudiates everything which the theogonic myth brings to mind from near or far. The theology of the Yahwistic and Priestly documents had already repudiated the theogonic myths which appear in Egyptian as well as in Assyrio-Babylonian and Phoenician religion. Christian theology, against the Gnostic mythologies of the first centuries, rejects the theogonic myth in all its forms. It will reject it again at the Vatican Council, this time against Hegel and Schelling.

The connection between the absolute and the world is

not therefore, according to Christianity, a connection of identity of substance (the world is not consubstantial with God), nor a necessary connection of eternal procession, or of emanation, or of logical explicitation, as theorems follow logically from a premise. The relationship between the absolute and the world according to Christianity is a relationship of freedom, which Hebrew and Christian theology expresses by the term creation. By this doctrine of creation we shall better understand what, or rather who, is the absolute according to Christianity.

As I have said, we are not taking into consideration in this present, synthetic account the historical order in which Christian metaphysics became progressively aware of itself. I may therefore quote, from the outset, very recent texts, namely, those of the first Vatican Council:

> The Holy Catholic Apostolic Roman Church believes that there is one true and living God, Creator and Lord of heaven and earth, omnipotent, eternal, immeasurable, incomprehensible, infinite in intellect and will and in every perfection; who, being one single, entirely simple and unchangeable spiritual substance, must be declared to be really and essentially distinct from the world, in himself and of himself most blessed and ineffably exalted above all things which are and which can be conceived outside him[1].

This text contains a certain number of propositions or

1 *Denz*, 1782; (Denzinger-Bannwart-Umberg-Rahner, *Enchiridion Symbolorum*, 31st edition, 1960).

assertions which are undeniably of a metaphysical order—
a single absolute (against polytheism and dualism), the
doctrine of the creation, the eternity of God, the distinction
between the absolute and the world, and others.

It may be thought that one seeks for metaphysical theses
in such a text. Surely it is beyond all question that these
theses are metaphysical, that they come of right within the
province of metaphysics, that they constitute a metaphysic
of the absolute by the same right as the doctrine of the
absolute according to Brahmanism, Aristotle, Plotinus,
Spinoza, Hegel, or any other philosopher.

Canons one to three relate to this first chapter:

1. If anyone denies (that there is) one true God,
Creator and Lord of things visible and invisible, let
him be anathema[2].
2. If anyone shamelessly affirms that outside matter
there is nothing, let him be anathema[3].
3. If anyone says that the substance or essence of
God and of all things is one and the same, let him be
anathema[4].

The first and second canons declare against atheism,
against, that is to say, a metaphysic which affirms that only
the material universe exists. Marxism is precisely in this
position. The first canon is intrinsically connected with the
second. To deny the existence of God amounts to saying

2 *Denz*, 1801.
3 *Denz*, 1802.
4 *Denz*, 1803.

that only the sensible world exists. The third and following canons declare against pantheism. We will find canons four and five in our next chapter, which is devoted to the relationship between the absolute and the world. We merely note here that to deny the existence of a creative and transcendant God amounts to affirming that the world is itself the absolute, since it is uncreated, ontologically sufficient, and, Marx adds, self-creative. The Fathers of the Vatican Council do not seem to have known, or to have had in direct view, the thought of Marx. They were alluding to the "materialism" which was known to them. But in fact, at the metaphysical level, these canons touch on the theses of Marx and Engels. Between materialism and pantheism there exist fundamental connections. Materialism, like pantheism, consists in affirming that the world is the absolute. For the materialist it is the absolute because it is uncreated, eternal, self-creative, infinite in space and in time, ontologically sufficient, furnished therefore with the classic attributes reserved to the absolute. On the metaphysical plane, materialism, and that of Marx in a singular manner, amounts to divinizing the cosmos. Pantheism on the contrary materializes and, if one may so put it, mundanizes the absolute. It describes a procession by which the absolute becomes nature by a fall or alienation. But materialism and pantheism—going in opposite directions—meet to affirm that the universe is the absolute, *natura sive Deus*. This is what Feuerbach discerned: "Atheism is the necessary outcome of pantheism, consistent pantheism". "Atheism is pantheism reversed".

We note here that in theological language materialism means precisely the doctrine which allows existence only to the material world, denying that there exists an absolute distinct from this world. Materialism is therefore practically synonymous with atheism. Christian thought does not, to be sure, deny the existence of matter—on the contrary indeed. Christian thought is not an idealism. But according to Christian philosophy, existing matter is not alone in existence and it is not uncreated; it is not ontologically sufficient. We will later state precisely, in an analogous manner, what is meant in theological language by rationalism. It is important to make very clear the use of these terms which in present-day language can be understood in a different sense.

From these solemn definitions and these canons it will be seen that one cannot speak of the doctrine of the absolute according to Christianity without calling to mind the doctrine of creation. The salient feature of the doctrine of the absolute, according to Judaism and according to Christianity, is that the absolute is not the world, that it is other than the world, and that the world is the creation of the absolute. It is in this very way that the absolute according to Christianity differentiates itself rrom the absolute according to Brahmanism and according to Plotinus or Spinoza. In our next chapter therefore we are going to meet again, or rather to state precisely, the doctrine of the absolute according to Christianity. As a matter of fact, without this doctrine of creation, there would be nothing to say about the absolute, according to Christianity. In other words, according to Christianity, the absolute is known only by creation, by its works, or at least and more exactly, by its creation. Without creation—and this is tautological —God would not be known.

CHAPTER TWO

The Relationships between the Absolute and the World— The Doctrine of Creation

FOR NEARLY TWO THOUSAND YEARS Christian thought has pondered this idea of creation. It can indeed be said that this meditation is of still earlier origin among the people of God, considering that the theological school, which produced the document called the Priestly Account by the critics, certain prophets such as the Deutero-Isaiah, the authors of certain psalms, and the inspired theologian, whom criticism calls the Yahwist, elaborated a doctrine of creation in terms of the preoccupations which were theirs, in terms, that is to say, of the oppositions which they encountered. Against the Egyptian and Assyrio-Babylonian mythologies the Hebrew theologians gradually formed a doctrine of creation which Christian thought has only had to take up again and to protect against the philosophies which challenged it. From the very beginnings, certain doctrines, philosophic and religious, have challenged this Jewish and Christian biblical idea of creation. Against Platonism, Aristotelianism, Stoicism, Neoplatonism, and the Gnostic systems, Christian thought has had to strive to save and to formulate its own doctrine of the creation. Again in the thirteenth century, Christian thought, faced with Neoplatonizing Aristotelianism and Arabian philosophies, had to defend its own theses. Against the pantheist systems of the Renaissance, and later against the systems of German idealism, Christian thought formulated its own theses.

Laboriously, in the course of the centuries, Christian thought had sifted out certain principles which we shall briefly summarize.

1. Creation is the work of an only God. There are not two creative absolutes, nor even two absolutes of whom one alone would be the creator. The single absolute is the creator. The creator of the world is not a sub-god, an inferior god, or an evil god. It is the only God, the God of Abraham, of Moses, and of Jesus who is the creator of heaven and earth. This replies to certain Gnostic and dualist systems.

2. Creation is free. God does not create from necessity. Creation is not a necessary and eternal procession, as for example in Plotinus or in Spinoza. Creation is not imposed upon God, either by an external necessity (destiny, fate) or by an internal necessity of development. Cosmogony is not theogony. God has no need to create the world to complete himself, to realize himself, to generate himself, to become aware of himself (a Gnostic and theosophical theme which is found again in Hegel). Creation is grace; it is the first grace, which Hugh of St. Victor called the *gratia creatrix*, which he distinguished from the *gratia salvatrix* and *reparatrix*. Creation is the work of the love of God. Christianity is a metaphysic of love. This point has been emphasized in a particularly profound manner by Fr. Laberthonnière.

3. Creation does not presuppose an uncreated and eternal matter on which the creator would have worked, which

he would have made use of as our workmen make use of matter to manufacture an object. Creation is not fabrication. The characteristic of creation, its originality, is precisely that there is no pre-existing matter, that God creates the matter also. Had there been pre-existing matter there would have been two absolutes, two uncreated principles, God and matter. This is contrary to Christian monotheism. God created matter; it is not eternal.

4. Creation is not an emanation of the divine substance, not a procession from the divine substance. Creation is not a generation. The created is not born of the divine substance, is not consubstantial with God. The Logos of God is consubstantial with God. It is not created, but begotten. We perceive the distinction between creation and generation. This distinction and the preceding distinction between creation and fabrication are summed up in the traditional proposition: creation is *ex nihilo*. In other words, it is not extracted from a pre-existing matter nor from the substance of God.

The doctrine of creation, virtually as old then as the manifestation of the living God to his people, is formulated by Christianity, following Judaism, in the New Testament and in the symbols of faith of the first centuries:

Creed of the Apostles: I believe in God, the father all-powerful, creator of heaven and earth[1].

Creed of the Apostles, oriental form: We believe in

1 *Denz*, 6.

one only God, father all-powerful, creator of heaven and earth, of all things visible and invisible[2].

Creed of Nicaea (325): We believe in one only God, father all-powerful, creator of all things visible and invisible[3].

It is known that the Creed of Nicaea is directed against theosophical systems according to which there are two principles, uncreated and in point of fact divine, of which one, the evil principle, is creator of the material world; whereas the other, the good principle, is either creator of nothing or else of souls only, but not of bodies or of matter.

First Council of Constantinople (2nd Ecumenical, 381):

We believe in one only God, father all-powerful, creator of heaven and earth, of all things visible and invisible[4].

Creed of the Council of Toledo, 400 and 447:

We believe in one true God, Father and Son and Holy Ghost, maker of the visible and the invisible, through whom were created all things in heaven and on earth[5].

2 *Denz*, 9.
3 *Denz*, 54.
4 *Denz*, 86.
5 *Denz*, 19.

The Council of Toledo was directed against the Priscillianists, who had adopted a metaphysic of a Manichean kind according to which the material, physical, corporeal world is not the work of the good God but the work of an evil principle. The Council of Toledo formulates a certain number of anathematizations which bear directly against this heresy concerning the creation:

1. If anyone says or believes that this world, together with all its elements, was not made by the omnipotent God, let him be anathema.
9. If anyone says or believes that the world was made by another God and not by him of whom it is written: *In the beginning God made heaven and earth*, let him be anathema.

Later on we shall meet the anathematizations of the Council of Toledo again, in connection with the doctrine of the soul.

Fourth Council of the Lateran (12th Ecumenical, 1215):

We firmly believe and simply confess that the true God is one only, eternal, immeasurable and unchangeable, incomprehensible, omnipotent and ineffable, Father and Son and Holy Ghost . . . ; the sole origin of all things, creator of all things visible and invisible, spiritual and corporeal; who by his omnipotent excellence formed out of nothing from the beginning of time at once both the spiritual creature and

the corporeal, that is to say the angelic and the
worldly, and thereafter the human, as if jointly constituted of spirit and body[6].

It is known that the profession of faith of the Fourth
Lateran Council struck at the dualist heresies which had
reappeared in the twelfth century. That is why the Council
insists on the fact that there is only one God (and not two
principles as absolute dualism taught) and that this single
God is creator of all, of material and corporeal as well as
spiritual nature. This latter point was made against the
same heresy, which taught that matter and the body are the
work of the evil god or (a qualified dualism) of a fallen
creature, Satan.

It must be noted here, in connection with this text, that
the Latin word *incomprehensibilis*, which we have translated as "incomprehensible", must be taken in its primary
sense—that which cannot be totally, exhaustively em-
braced by the intellect, or fully possessed and used up by a
created thought.

In the general session of the Council of Florence, held
on February 4, 1442, union was concluded with the Jaco-
bites and the decree of union, *Cantate Domino*, contains a
statement of the Catholic Faith. Let us consider what this
17th Ecumenical Council has to say regarding the doctrine
of creation.

The Sacrosanct Roman Church, founded by the
voice of our lord and Saviour, firmly believes, pro-

6 *Denz*, 428.

fesses and preaches one true, omnipotent God, unchangeable and eternal, Father and Son and Holy
Ghost.

She firmly believes, professes and preaches that the
one true God, Father and Son and Holy Ghost, is the
creator of all things visible and invisible; who, when
he willed, out of his goodness, formed all creatures
both spiritual and corporeal; good indeed (he made
them) because they were made by the supreme good,
but changeable because they were made out of nothing; and she declares that there is no nature of evil
because all nature, in so far as it is nature, is good.

She anathematizes the madness of the Manicheans
who have posited two first principles, one of things
visible and the other of things invisible[7].

In addition to the traditional teaching about the creation,
this text contains some new notes. It teaches the freedom of
the creation: God created when he wished to. He created of
his goodness, not out of a necessity which would have been
imposed on him. The creature, as such, is good because it
comes from him who is the supreme good. It is changeable,
by construction, because it is not born of the divine substance, is not consubstantial with God, but is created out of
nothing. We have here then a doctrine concerning evil
which is that of Augustine. In contrast to the Manichean
position, there is no evil nature; there is no nature of evil.
Again we meet the doctrine of Augustine. All nature, as it

7 *Denz*, 703 and 706.

is, is good, an Augustinian axiom. The Council of Florence rejects, once more, the dualism of principles.

It will be seen how the Christian doctrine of creation implies a doctrine of evil which is equally original. Evil is not a substance, or a nature. Evil is not an uncreated principle co-eternal with God. No creature is, as such, evil. Evil arises from human freedom (our text does not explicitly refer to this); and if this freedom is fallible, it is because it is created out of nothing and is not yet stablized, confirmed, in the ultimate beatitude.

Farther on, the same Bull, *Cantate Domino*, professes afresh this ontological optimism with regard to creation. *Firmiter credit, profitetur et praedicat, omnem creaturam Dei bonam, nihilque rejiciendum, quod cum gratiarum actione percipitur* (I Tim. 4:4)[8].

Vatican Council, 1870, constitution on the Catholic Faith, cap. 1. *De Deo rerum omnium creatore:*

> This one true God, by his goodness and omnipotent excellence, not to augment or add to his beatitude, but to manifest his perfection by the good things which he imparts to creatures, by entirely free design formed out of nothing from the beginning of time at once both the spiritual creature and the corporeal, that is to say, the angelic and the worldly, and thereafter the human, as if jointly constituted of spirit and body[9].

With this second paragraph of the first chapter of the

8 *Denz,* 713.
9 *Denz,* 1783.

constitution *De Fide* Canons three, four, and five are connected.

> Canon 3: If anyone says that the substance or essence of God and of all things is one and the same, let him be anathema[10].
> Canon 4: If anyone says that finite things, be they corporeal or be they spiritual or, at least, the spiritual have emanated from the divine substance;
>
> or that the divine essence, by manifestation or evolution of itself, becomes all things;
>
> or finally that God is a universal or undefined being which, by determining itself constitutes the universality of things divided into genera, species and individuals, let him be anathema[11].
> Canon 5: If anyone does not acknowledge that the world and all things which are contained therein, both spiritual and material, have been produced by God out of nothing in the totality of their substance;
>
> or says that God did not create by a will free from all necessity but that he created as necessarily as he necessarily loves himself;
>
> or denies that the world was established for the glory of God, let him be anathema[12].

This second paragraph of the first chapter of the constitution *De Fide* and its adjoining canons set forth the Chris-

10 *Denz*, 1803.
11 *Denz*, 1804.
12 *Denz*, 1805.

tian doctrine of creation, in opposition to the various philosophies which were unaware of it, denied it, or deformed
it.

Creation is the work of the goodness of God. Its purpose
is not to augment the bliss of God or to permit him to
acquire a perfection which he would not already have. This
first proposition aims at the theogonic myth which dwells in
Gnostic and theosophical speculations in the first centuries
of the Christian era, and also in more recent philosophies,
such as those which flourished in Germany at the beginning
of the nineteenth century. Cosmogony is in no way theogony. God does not create in order to realize himself, to
achieve himself. God has no need to create to realize and
become aware of himself. It is in German idealism, last of
all, in Hegel most especially, that this theogonic myth finds
extreme and amazing expression. It is against the doctrines
born of German idealism that the Fathers of the Vatican
Council direct their definitions. The creation manifests the
perfection of God, a manifestation gracious, free, and of
the divine generosity. At the beginning of all things there is
the *agape* of God. This is the theme which Fr. Laberthonnière developed all his life and which constitutes the principle of what he called "the metaphysic of charity". The
creation is free on the part of God; it is not imposed on him
by any necessity, internal or external. The creation is not a
necessary procession from the divine nature. It does not
respond to any necessity imposed from without. Neither
does it respond to an internal need of realization. It is a
giving, an act of grace.

It is by this, in this, that the Christian metaphysic of

creation differentiates itself fundamentally from the Plotinian doctrine of procession, from the philosophy of Spinoza, and from the Hegelian theogony.

Canons three, four, and five strike directly at these various forms of pantheism. The creature is not consubstantial with the Creator; the soul is not a small fragment of the divine substance; nature is not absolute mind alienated; the creation of beings is not a procession analogous to that of rays of light which emanate from a luminous source or of heat which emanates from a burning body. Physical nature is not a petrifaction of the divine substance. In the thought of the Council Fathers Canon four strikes most particularly at Fichte, Schelling, and Hegel. Canon five strikes more directly at the doctrines of Gunther and d'Hermès.

In the paragraph quoted of the chapter which we have just read, the Fathers of the Vatican Council have reproduced the text of the Fourth Lateran Council which we have previously read, and in which there is question of the "beginning of time", *ab initio temporis*.

It is necessary to recall here that in the chapters of a constitution promulgated by an Ecumenical Council, it is advisable, from the theological point of view as well as from the metaphysical, to distinguish between what the Fathers of the Council have in view (what they wish to define, or, more exactly, what they wish to preserve, to protect, their intention), and their language, their representations, their way of expressing themselves. These latter can be bound up with a given culture, with a given vision of the world, with a state of knowledge in a given period, and for that very reason can constitute a veneer which is possibly decayed. One cannot therefore take the chapters of an Ecumenical Council as the geometrician takes propositions from which he makes mathematical deductions. One must ask in the first place what doctrine the Fathers of the Council wish to repel. By virtue of this, the canon of a Council and its anathematizations in an apophatic manner define more exactly the intention, the aim of the Council, what it wishes to repel and refuse, and what, in the same way, it wishes to protect and save in the thought of the Church.

In other words, one cannot treat the chapters of a conciliar definition as the cabalists treat the sacred texts of Scripture. In the exegesis of conciliar texts, as in that of Holy Scripture, scientific method is required in order to avoid both misinterpretations and faulty deductions.

Here then, in our paragraph, following the Lateran Council, the Fathers of the Vatican Council express the traditional thought of the Church: creation has a beginning. No anathematization condemns the contrary proposition, because doubtless no school of theology since Origen has professed an eternal creation or a creation eternally renewed, save perhaps Meister Eckhart.

Sacred Scripture teaches that the creation has had a beginning. "In the beginning God created heaven and earth". But one can, with Origen, ask oneself whether this beginning relates to creation itself or merely to this world. One can imagine that this world may have had a temporal beginning, although creation itself may be eternal. Before this world God would have created other worlds; after this world God would continue to create others. This is the thesis maintained in the *De Principiis* by Origen. One could, from an abstract point of view, maintain that this hypothesis of an eternal creation is not, taken in itself and formally, in absolute and necessary contradiction with Christian dogma. At least we do not see for the moment where the incompatibility lies, if one maintains the essential liberty of God in the creative act, and if one does not make of the creation a procession co-eternal with God because it is involved in a necessary manner in his nature.

From the point of view of concrete experience, we must note that all beings begin to exist. This being so, how could the universe be without beginning? Living species, complex matter, pre-living matter, all have, in the universe, a certain age; all have a date of birth. If we speak of the eternity of the universe, of the eternity of matter, of what matter do we speak? Of the atom of hydrogen? This, in its complex structure, does not escape temporariness; it too has a certain age. Of what matter is one speaking when one imagines an eternity of matter?

St. Thomas, we know, distinguished very precisely between the idea of creation and the idea of beginning. To say that the world is created is not the same thing as to say that it has a beginning. One can, in the first approach and abstractly, in a formal fashion, say that the world is created without expressing one's opinion on the question of knowing whether it began to be or whether it is eternal. A world conceived as eternal, as Aristotle conceived it, could still be a created world. The idea of creation signifies a relationship of dependence. But to reason thus formally (*semper formaliter loquitur divus Thomas*), to philosophize about the reality existing in fact, is another matter. In fact, and from the point of view of our experience as it is known today, to speak of an eternal universe has little meaning. In St. Thomas Aquinas's day one could still ask oneself whether living species were not eternal; we know today that living species are temporal. We have no need to demonstrate this. Fossils point it out to us. We know likewise that matter, be it uranium or lead, carbon or nucleoproteins, is temporal.

But it remains possible to suppose an eternal creation, that is to say a creation which will eternally renew beings and things. The concrete matter which we know in our experience is certainly not eternal, but one can suppose a creation eternally begun over again from ever new matter. This is the hypothesis of a contemporary astro-physicist, Fred Hoyle. In a hypothesis of this sort all beings, in particular, begin to exist, but the totality, the whole, the universe can be conceived as eternal—like Peter's knife, of which now the haft is changed, now the blade, and which remains Peter's knife despite all that. Our perspective would thus be more Heraclitan than Aristotelian. For Aristotle it is really this universe which is eternal, because it is divine.

Let us conclude. Scripture and experience teach us that the universe is temporal, and that everything began to exist. But abstractly, at least, and in the present state of our knowledge, both physical and theological, nothing, it seems, prevents us from conceiving as possible a creation eternally renewed. The only drawback, from the theological point of view, makes itself evident in a collation of a depiction of this sort with the Christian doctrine of the pleroma. The pleroma, the Kingdom of God, would according to this hypothesis be eternally contemporaneous, if one can so put it, with a birth and painful parturition of souls in a system of creation. The blissful eternity of perfected beings would already be realized, while on the other hand worlds would be engaged in bringing themselves to birth.

From the first centuries of the Christian era, the Fathers of the Church have had to struggle against the Platonic and Aristotelian idea of an eternal world. In the sixth century John Philoponos in opposition to Aristotle dedicated a treatise to the problem of the eternity of the world. But it was in the thirteenth century particularly that debate began in this field between Christian philosophy and the Aristotelian philosophy which the Arabs brought to the West.

Christian thought in the thirteenth century, faced with a rising tide of Neoplatonizing Aristotelianism brought in by the Arabs, went through a crisis of belief which was most important from the metaphysical point of view. Among the theses condemned by the bishop of Paris, Étienne Tempier, in 1270 and 1277, there appear some doctrines which are properly cosmological, and which are in fact bound up with a certain ontology. The fifth error condemned by Étienne Tempier, in 1270, is the Aristotelian and Averroist doctrine of the eternity of the world, *quod mundus est aeternus*. In 1277 as well, several of the condemned theses bear on the eternity of the world[13].

In 1329, John XXII condemned several propositions attributed to Meister Eckhart and worded as follows:

1. Questioned once as to why God had not produced the world sooner, he responded then as now that God was not able to produce the world sooner because a thing cannot act before it is; from which it follows that as soon as God existed he created the world[14].

2. In like manner it is possible to concede that the world existed from eternity[15].

3. In like manner at once and at a single time, when God was, when he begat his Son, God, co-eternal with him and co-equal in all things, he also created the world[16].

13 *Cf.* "Propositions condamnées par Étienne Tempier", in Mandonnet, *Siger de Brabant et l'averroisme latin*, 11, Louvain 1911, 182-3.
14 *Denz*, 501.
15 *Denz*, 502.
16 *Denz*, 503.

CHAPTER THREE

The Cosmic System— World Structure

ONE SEES that in fact, whether we wish it or not, we are led towards cosmological matters. Between metaphysics, theology, cosmology, and anthropology there exist relationships which are not accidental. For well-defined organic reasons any metaphysic whatever is not compatible with any theology whatever. Any cosmology whatever, any anthropology whatever is not compatible with any metaphysic. From this we may conclude that any cosmology whatever and any anthropology whatever are not compatible with any theology whatever. Pierre Duhem, in his magistral *Système du Monde*, has clearly shown the relationships which exist between these different orders. The disputes about the eternity or noneternity of the world, which never cease from the first Christian centuries up to the Middle Ages, plainly demonstrate that Christian thought, like Jewish and Moslem thought also, was aware of these relationships and involvements. The disputes regarding the relations between anthropology and Christology—with regard to Apollinaris, for example—also clearly prove that any anthropology whatever is not compatible with Christology, just as the disputes about Origenism prove that any doctrine whatever of soul and body is not compatible with Christianity. But this is another question we shall meet again later.

Because relationships exist between theology, metaphysics, and cosmology, we are inevitably brought face to face with a group of problems which revolve around what has been called "concordism". "Concordism" was an attempt to make agree what did not agree—the data of the positive sciences concerning geological and biological evolution, and the account in Genesis. It is said that there is "concordism" when the one and the other are not in concord. The anti-concordist reaction, which was largely healthy and legitimate, failed nevertheless to recognize the intrinsic relationships which exist between theology, metaphysics, cosmology, and the positive sciences. It would be no recommendation for metaphysics if that science had no relationship with the positive sciences, if metaphysical reflection was absolutely independent of the experimental and scientific order. That would prove that metaphysics had no relation to reality. If, as we endeavor to show, Christian theology comprises a certain metaphysical structure, it follows inevitably that between theology and cosmology, between theology and the positive sciences, certain relationships exist.

In point of fact, Christian theology holds itself to be incompatible with a vision of the world which would assert that the universe was eternal and imperishable. In point of fact, Sacred Scripture comprises a certain cosmology, a certain doctrine of the world, not simply at the level of the childish representations of ancient man but, more profoundly, at a level close to ontology. For an Aristotle, the stars were uncreated substances, imperishable and eternal. For Hebraic and Jewish thought, the stars are created and perishable things. For an Aristotle, the stars represented consistency itself, eternal stability. For a Hebrew, God will roll up the sky as a carpet is rolled up in the East. The stars will be shaken down like the fruit of a plum-tree. The earth too will be shaken; the hills will bound like sheep. The world, from the Hebrew point of view, is not stability. The "Rock", Stability, is Yahweh. He only is eternal, constant, permanent. The world is fragile. From this one example we see how a cosmology can have ontological implications and, inversely, how an ontology can have cosmological consequences.

Christianity has inherited this ontology and this cosmology. Christianity professes the beginning and the end of the world. That is a properly cosmological affirmation, which in its principal direction at the very least, is answerable to the positive sciences. It is an affirmation which shocks the Aristotelian philosopher, and, in our day, the Marxist philosopher.

According to orthodox Christianity then, matter, physical reality, is created. It is not eternal, nor ontologically sufficient. Neither is it the work of an evil principle, as in the Manichean system. Matter is therefore a reality excellent in its order, and no bad conscience should trouble the Christian because of it. Evil is not an effect of materiality. It is the work of human freedom.

There follows from this cosmology a certain doctrine of the temporal. Much has been written on this subject in recent years and therefore we shall not dwell on it. It has been said that Christian time was linear, whereas Hellenic time was cyclic. To say that time is linear is obviously an unfortunate expression, since time is precisely not spatial. But what remains correct, under the unhappy term, is that Christian time measures a creation irreversibly directed towards a unique and definitive end. Christian time is vectorial. It measures a ripening which will find an eternal completion. This vision of things is clearly contrary to any *Weltanschauung* which propounds an eternal re-commencement of the cosmic cycle.

CHAPTER FOUR

Anthropology

THE DOCTRINE OF TEMPORALITY is in fact bound up with an anthropology, in this way: the Christian doctrine of irreversible and orientated temporality is linked with the idea of a beginning of existence, for particular beings as well as for the whole. We have begun to exist, recently. The idea of temporality is linked with the idea of beginning, as it is also linked with the idea of change, which Bergson has shown. Now in a number of metaphysical systems the soul is declared to be eternal, is stated to be pre-existent to its coming into the body. Birth does not really represent a beginning of existence but merely the emergence, at the level of appearances, of a soul which already existed. In this view there is no beginning of existence, nor, moreover, is there death. This is what is expressly put into words by many texts of the Upanishad, of the Bhagavad-Gita, and of Empedocles besides. The soul is eternal and uncreated. It does not begin to exist. The Christian doctrine of temporality, on the contrary, expresses the fact that a continued creation places in existence beings which did not previously exist in any way. Biblical tradition is entirely unaware of the theme of the pre-existence of the soul, as it is unaware

71

of the theme of transmigration; Christian tradition formally rejects this theme whenever it meets it. We perceive therefore the intimate relationship which exists between the doctrine of time and anthropology.

Christian anthropology defines itself first and foremost by a proposition parallel to that which we have already called to mind in connection with cosmology—man is created. The human soul is not a particle or fragment, nor is it a modality of the divine substance. The human soul is created; it is a creature. By this fundamental, metaphysical thesis Christian thought repudiated one of the most constant themes in the thought of ancient India and of ancient Greece.

The soul is created; it is not pre-existent to its body; it does not pass from body to body; it has not fallen into a body which is supposed to be evil. It is created in a corporeal condition, in other words, as experience shows, through the union of two cells which constitute a new being at once material and psychic, provided with interiority and sensibility, and later with reflexive consciousness and liberty. That two material cells coming from two beings can form a single subject is a datum of common experience worthy of prolonged meditation on the part of the metaphysician. But this is not the place to indulge in it.

Biblical tradition, and Christian tradition in its wake, do not regard corporality as an evil, or as a falling place for the soul, but as the normal condition of the created, living being. As we have noted, just as biblical tradition and Christian philosophy are unaware of any bad conscience with regard to matter (physical reality), so also, and for the same reasons, they are unaware of any bad conscience where corporality is concerned. And that has not been without merit. For Christian thought has been literally assailed by the Gnostic and dualist streams of thought. It has protected itself with desperate eagerness against this temptation; it has hurled it far from itself in solemn condemnations, directed against the Gnostics of the first centuries, against the Manicheans, against the Origenists, against the Priscillianists, and then against the Neomanicheans in the Middle Ages. It is therefore through a major misunderstanding that theses and tendencies are sometimes ascribed to Christianity which Christianity has unceasingly repudiated and condemned.

The Council of Toledo, in the year 400, in its rule of faith against all heresies and in particular against the Priscillianists, laid down that "the soul of man is not a divine substance, nor a part of God, but is a creature", *animam autem hominis non divinam esse substantiam, aut Dei partem, sed creaturam*[1]. The eleventh anathematization of the same Council condemns the Manichean doctrine revived by the Priscillianists:

"If anyone says and (or) believes that the human soul is a portion of God, or is the substance of God, let him be anathema"[2].

In 543, the Synod of Constantinople, over which the Patriarch Menas presided, promulgates, against the Origenist doctrines, some canons proposed by the Emperor Justinian and probably confirmed by Pope Vigilius. These canons

1 *Denz*, 20.
2 *Denz*, 31.

condemn the doctrine—which is orphic, Platonic, and Neoplatonic as much as Gnostic—of the pre-existence of the soul and its fall into an evil body.

Canon 1: If anyone says or thinks that the souls of men pre-exist, inasmuch as they were formerly intellects and holy powers and became satiated with divine contemplation and were changed for the worse, and for that reason grew cold in the love of God, because of which they were called souls, and were thrust down into bodies for punishment, let him be anathema[3].

In 553, a special Council held at Constantinople resumes the same condemnations:

If anyone subscribes to the mythical doctrine of the pre-existence of souls ... let him be anathema.

In 561, the Council of Braga, directed against the Priscillianists, condemns the Manichean doctrine according to which souls would be drawn out of the substance of God and would be therefore consubstantial with God, and the Origenist and Gnostic doctrine of the pre-existence and fall of souls into evil bodies:

Canon 5: If anyone believes that human souls or the angels came forth out of the substance of God, as Manichaeus and Priscillian said, let him be anathema[4].

3 Denz, 203.
4 Denz, 235.

Canon 6: If anyone says that human souls sinned previously in a celestial abode and were on that account cast into human bodies on earth, as Priscillian said, let him be anathema[5].

The Fourth Council of Constantinople (8th Ecumenical), in 869-870 condemns the doctrine according to which man would have two souls:

Whereas the Old and New Testaments teach that man has a single rational and intellectual soul, and all the divinely instructed Fathers and teachers of the Church strongly assert the same belief, certain persons, devoting themselves to evil inventions have arrived at such a degree of impiety that they impudently try to teach that man has two souls and to support their heresy by certain irrationalities . . . Therefore this holy and ecumenical Council strongly anathematizes the inventors and perpetrators of such an impiety and all who think like them . . .[6]

Leo IX, in his *Symbolum fidei* of 1053, continues the firm teaching of the Church which had been formulated against Manicheism: the soul is not a fragment of God; it is created, *animam non esse partem Dei, sed ex nihilo creatam.*

In the thirteenth century, in 1270 and 1277, the Bishop of Paris, faced with the invading tide of Neoplatonizing

5 *Denz*, 236.
6 *Denz*, 338.

Aristotelianism and by order moreover of the Pope, condemned as we have already seen a certain number of
theses. Some among these concern anthropology. They
take up, and transpose, the Neoplatonic monopsychism of
which the most marvelous expression is found in Plotinus.
The first proposition condemned in 1270 is that of the
unity of the intellect in all men, *Quod intellectus omnium
hominum est unus et idem numero.* Likewise, in 1277,
Étienne Tempier had to condemn the propositions according to which God could not create several souls, *Quod Deus
non posset facere plures animas in numero,* and the intellect would be one for all men, *Quod intellectus est unus
numero omnium*[7].

The Council of Vienne (15th Ecumenical, 1311-1312),
defined, against Petrus Joannis Olivi, that the soul is the
form of the body without intermediary:

> Further, with the approval of the said Sacred
> Council we reject as erroneous and opposed to the
> truth of the Catholic faith any doctrine or any thesis
> which rashly affirms, or leaves open to doubt, that the
> substance of the rational or intellectual soul is not
> truly and of itself the form of the human body; and we
> define, so that all may know the truth of the pure faith
> and that the door may be closed against all errors lest
> they should creep in, that anyone henceforth who will
> have presumed to affirm, defend or obstinately hold
> that the rational or intellectual soul is not of itself

7 Cf. Mandonnet, *op. cit.* 184.

and essentially the form of the human body, is to be considered a heretic[8].

In 1329, John XXII condemns a proposition attributed to Eckhart and worded as follows:

> There is something in the soul which is uncreated and uncreatable; if the entire soul were such, it would be uncreated and uncreatable, and this is the intellect[9].

In 1341, Benedict XII condemns a number of errors ascribed to the Armenians. Among these errors we find the following:

> A certain master of the Armenians called Mechitriz, which means Paraclete, introduced a new teaching to the effect that the human soul of the son is propagated by the soul of his father, as the body is by the body; and also one angel by another; because, the human soul being of a rational nature and the angel being of an intellectual nature, they are so to speak spiritual lights and they propagate out of themselves other spiritual lights[10].

In 1513, the Fifth Lateran Council (18th Ecumenical), in its eighth session rejects the doctrine of the "neo-Aristo-

8 *Denz*, 481.
9 *Denz*, 527.
10 Mansi, *Sacrorum Conciliorum Collectio*, xxv, col. 1193.

telians" of the school of Padua and of Pietro Pomponazzi
in particular, according to which the soul would be one
only, for all men. On the other hand, the individual as such
would not have a future. One recognizes afresh a Plotinian
thesis: the universal soul is one only; each individual soul is
a fragment of the universal soul which is as a matter of fact
divine. Individuation is the result of a negative process,
fall, and embodiedness. Salvation consists in liberating oneself from this unhappy individuation and from this embodiedness by which the universal soul is exiled, impris-
oned, and, as it were, limited and restricted in a particular
body. The Church rejects this doctrine:

> Since in our days—we speak of it with difficulty—
> the sower of tares, the ancient enemy of mankind,
> has dared to sow and multiply in the field of the Lord
> some most dangerous errors which have always been
> rejected by the faithful, concerning especially the
> nature of the rational soul, to the effect that it is
> mortal or one only in all men; and some, rashly phi-
> losophizing, assert this to be true according to phi-
> losophy at least; being desirous of employing oppor-
> tune remedies against a pestilence of this kind, with
> the approval of this sacred Council we condemn and
> disapprove of all who assert that the intellectual soul
> is mortal or is one only in all men, and all who doubt
> on this point, since not only is the soul truly of itself
> and essentially the form of the human body, as in the
> terms of the canon of our predecessor, Pope Clement
> V of happy memory, given forth at the General

Council of Vienne, but it is also immortal and in view of the multitude of bodies into which it is infused, is individually multipliable, is multiplied and must be multiplied[11].

In 1687, Innocent XI condemns certain propositions of Miguel de Molinos. We draw attention to one among them which seems indeed to assert that the soul is of divine essence in its primary basis.

By being busied with nothing the soul annihilates itself and returns to its principle and to its origin, which is the essence of God, in which it abides transformed and divinized, and God then abides in himself; for then there are no longer two things united, but one thing only[12].

These several condemnations and definitions converge to rule out certain metaphysical theses, and at the same time, in an apophatic fashion, to protect and surround a positive doctrine concerning anthropology, that of Christianity.

Let us recapitulate. The soul is not of divine essence; it is not a particle or a modality of the divine substance. It is really created. By this the traditional doctrines of Brahmanism, Orphism, Platonism, and the Neoplatonism of the Gnosis, as well as Spinozism, are dismissed.

The soul is not pre-existent to the body. The living body exists as a living body only because it is animated. A body

11 *Denz*, 738.
12 *Denz*, 1225.

without the soul is no longer a body but a heap, a multiplicity of biochemical elements which is called a corpse and which retains merely the appearance of a body, temporarily. The soul is the "form" which unifies this multiplicity of integrated biochemical elements. It constitutes the body as such. It is united with matter to constitute a living body. Christian thought rejects therefore the traditional doctrines according to which the soul would be pre-existent to the body. It rejects the substantial dualism which makes one substance of the soul and another of the body. The living body is the synthesis of a living soul and matter which it unifies and informs. In the same way Christian thought rejects all bad conscience and all condemnation as far as the body is comcerned. The body is not something other than the man. The body is not a stranger to the man. Man is also a body. One cannot therefore lay upon the body the responsibility for faults or weaknesses which are the business of the whole man.

By these definitions Christian thought attests its fidelity to the principles of biblical anthropology.

Orthodox Christian thought rejects also the doctrine according to which the human soul would be transmitted, if one can so put it, by the parents, propagated by the parents as if it were a material thing which can cut itself up, a material substance of which one can furnish a portion. Two living cells coming from two parents constitute, in uniting, a new and autonomous organism which is also a subject, a living and spiritual soul. The materiality of two cells is not sufficient to account for this real creation of a subject, ontologically distinct from the parents. Orthodox Christian thought, following biblical thought, discerns, in the conception of a child from two cells which come from the parents, a genuine and complete creation which can only have God himself for its author, directly. Having rejected the mythical doctrine of the pre-existence of the soul, Christian thought considers that creation continues at the time of the conception of a child, following in this the text in the Gospel of St. John (5:17): "My Father has never ceased working, and I too must be at work". This text was invoked in connection with this very question by St. Jerome in his discussion with St. Augustine. It is God, the unique Creator, who acts at the time of each conception, using second causes, even within the second causes which are, in the circumstances, the parents. The parents are the active instruments, the co-operators, in a work of creation which in fact transcends them.

Christian thought has, lastly, rejected Neoplatonic monopsychism, which is in fact akin to pantheism, since the unique soul, in which we would be only particles or modalities, is, according to Plotinus and according to the whole Neoplatonic tradition, a universal divine soul. Christian thought has upheld the ontological distinction between created subjects and the Neoplatonism which expresses itself in the Enneads of Plotinus, Siger de Brabant in the thirteenth century, later in the philosophers of the School of Padua, and later still in Spinoza.

CHAPTER FIVE

Human Nature

IN THEIR MOST PROFOUND AND ESSENTIAL IMPULSE, biblical tradition and Christian tradition have had a steadfast tendency to exalt human nature, to magnify and develop it, up to and including, as we shall see later, a "foolish" hope, an unparalleled, properly supernatural hope—divinization.

"Thou hast made him a little less than the angels, thou hast crowned him with glory and honour. Thou hast set him over the works of thy hands, thou hast subjected all things under his feet". According to Christianity man is not, by nature, of divine essence; he is not a divine soul fallen into an evil body, but is called to divinization; he is, by creation, prepared for and pre-adapted to this supernatural end. Human nature is pre-adapted to its supernatural end. Creation is a free act. Divinization is also free; it is a giving of grace. Everything, in the work of God, is grace. But the gifts of God are interconnected; there is a certain convergence, an economy. The gifts of God do not follow after one another, do not superimpose themselves in a discontinuous fashion like whimsical edicts. They are linked to one another; they call to one another; they prepare for one another. Yet there is never any occasion to take from the freedom and gratuitousness of the giving. There is thus in human nature a pre-adaption to its supernatural end, which it is permissible for the philosopher to examine and analyze. It is this pre-adaptation which makes man *capax Dei*, which willingly puts us in touch with the *desiderium naturale sed inefficax videndi Deum*.

Steadfastly and unwearyingly, orthodox Christian tradition has defended human nature against those who tended to degrade, despise, and diminish it.

1. Against the Gnostic and Manichean systems, against Neoplatonism and Origenism, against mediaeval dualism, orthodox Christian tradition has firmly maintained the excellence in its order of the corporeal nature of man. God has created man corporeal. Man is not a soul fallen into an evil body. The corporeal, corporality, is created by the same unique Creator and not by an evil god or perverse principle. Corporality was not given to man because of sin or in anticipation of sin—contrary to Origen and Gregory of Nyssa. In my work on the birth of Christian philosophy I have analyzed the myth of the fall of the soul under its various forms and in its various avatars—in Indian thought, in Orphism, in Platonism, in Neoplatonism, in the Gnosis, in Origenism. Let us simply recall here that orthodox Christian thought has constantly rejected, repelled, and condemned the inherent tendencies towards all these systems; and one may almost say that, in part, orthodoxy defines and characterizes itself by this rejection. Corporality is neither an accident nor a catastrophe. It is in the creative plan of God. Matter is not a place of fall, or a blemish, or a place of exile. It is a creature excellent in its order, *materia*

matrix, as Fr. Teilhard de Chardin says. In the twelfth century orthodox Christian thought, faced with the Manichean renewal, repeated its censures of these same tendencies. Nothing therefore is more firmly established than this doctrine of the excellence of the material, of the corporeal, of physical reality.

2. More particularly where sexuality is concerned, it must be recalled that biblical tradition is entirely free of all bad conscience or feeling of guilt with regard to sexuality. On the contrary (as I have pointed out elsewhere), the theosophical and metaphysical tradition of India, Orphism, Plato, and Plotinus, the Gnostics and the Manicheans, all regard sexuality as an evil; sexuality and desire are indeed doubly responsible for embodiedness, for the fall of souls into the body. It is by desire that the soul is plunged into the material, and it is procreation which makes blissful souls fall into bodies. Sexuality, according to these various traditions, is fall. It is very probable that the whole doctrine of matter and corporality in these different systems proceeds, psychologically, from this original aversion from sexuality.

Christian thought, in the first centuries and up to the present day, has been tempted by this emotional, negative attitude to sexuality, and consequently to corporality. We have seen it in Origen and in Gregory of Nyssa. But in St. Basil also, in St. Jerome, and in St. Augustine, one can easily detect an unresolved conflict regarding sexuality. Origen regards corporality, and consequently sexuality, as a consequence of the original fall of pure, bare, spiritual substances. According to Gregory of Nyssa sexuality was granted to corporeal creatures only in anticipation of original sin. In God's primary plan reproduction was meant to be angelic. St. Jerome could not help advising against marriage as much as possible, because of what he deemed to be its turpitudes. For St. Augustine also, who concedes that in Paradise reproduction would have been sexual, it is still true that the union of man and woman would not have been emotionally passionate as it is today. What shocks St. Augustine deeply is what he calls the involuntary movements of the flesh, that is to say the normal reflexes of sexuality. He admits with difficulty this spontaneity of the biological order, independent of the reason. He identifies original sin with concupiscence. This latter, moreover, for St. Augustine, goes far beyond the domain of sex. For him sexuality is thus connected in a profound way with original sin.

What is very remarkable is that orthodox thought in its development and in its solemn decisions did not adopt these tendencies, which meanwhile were to be found in some of the most considerable inclinations of the Fathers of the Church. The Church has rejected Origenism. It has always maintained the sanctity of marriage, and has denied the identification of original sin with concupiscence despite the authority of Augustine. One sees by this example how the thought of the Church is free where its Doctors are concerned; it is independent of the greatest of them; it is autonomous. It was the error of Jansenism to depend in a unilateral fashion on certain texts of St. Augustine when the thought of the Church is collective. What is essential to sift out, in order to know this thought, is a consensus, a convergence, a profound agreement between all the Doctors. The authority of one, however great he be, does not suffice to determine it.

In the Middle Ages, against the Catharist heresies, the Church resumed its struggle against the systems which regarded matter, corporality, sexuality, as born of the evil, diabolic principle and which in consequence prohibited marriage and procreation.

In spite of this constant battle against a Manichean type of dualism, it remains latent, more or less implicit, obscure, in a number of Christian consciences. One recognizes its traces (traces, in the chemists' usage), in a sermon or in a work of spirituality, in a way of behavior or in a reflex action. Manicheism is certainly one of the hidden heresies which is rife in Christendom. It is one of the heresies which most distorts Christianity today, since non-Christians, those on the outside, upbraid Christianity, as often as not, for trends and theses which they believe they see in Christendom and which are in fact typically Manichean trends and doctrines.

Much of this heresy remains, although in its general tendencies the modern world (which rejects and, one may say, vomits all that is left of Manicheism in Western tradition, in rightly claiming the excellence of the corporeal), fails to recognize that sexuality, though certainly not sin in itself, is nevertheless a privileged place of sin, an important point of application of human sin. Therefore, in conformity with orthodox Christian tradition, the excellence of the corporeal as such, the excellence of the created instincts, must be maintained; in conformity with the great ascetical and mystical tradition the excellence of ascesis, which is necessary because of sin, must also be maintained.

Continence, writes St. Thomas, would not in the state of innocence have been a praiseworthy thing (*Summa Theologica*, 1, quaest. xcviii, art.ii, ad 3um). But it has become such because of sin, because of the world, which has a vital need of this testimony to liberty, as it has a vital need of the testimony of voluntary and agreed poverty and of nonviolence.

In the first centuries of the Christian era, orthodoxy had above all to fight against those Gnostic systems and Neoplatonic philosophies which we have called to mind. Later, Christian thought would have to fight against doctrines which challenged in a profound and subtle fashion the excellence and integrity of human nature. The two principal points on which the conflicts turned are on the one hand the doctrine of freedom and on the other the doctrine of reason.

On the first point, the doctrine of freedom, orthodox Christian tradition from the beginnings of Christian thought is unanimous. That very destiny which is proposed for man, the destiny of a god called to participate in the very life of God, implies and presupposes that man is a free entity. Man has been created in the image and likeness of God. How would that be possible if man were not a free entity, responsible for and creative of his works? Divinization cannot be imposed on man in such a way that he receives it in a completely passive fashion. The dignity of man, his destiny as a god, implies that he co-operates in this genesis which is his own, in the anthropo-genesis which will perfect itself by a theo-genesis. This is the basis of that claim for the creative dignity of man of which expression is found in many an intellectual movement since the Renaissance and in particular in our own day in Marxism. It answers to a profoundly legitimate and healthy demand.

In the anti-Manichean controversy Augustine, together with all the Fathers who were obliged to intervene, defends human liberty against a doctrine which regards man as fallen, in consequence of a mythical theomachy, into matter and into an evil body. It is not therefore man who would be responsible for the evil which he does. It is matter, an evil principle, eternal, uncreated, co-eternal with God, holding prisoner the sparks sprung from the divine substance. When man does evil he can therefore according to this system say, "It is not I, it is my body, it is matter which are responsible". Against the Manicheans Augustine asserted the full responsibility of man. Evil is not the act of human nature but of human freedom.

On the other hand, in his struggle against Pelagianism Augustine had to insist above all on the priority of grace. God is first in the act of creation and in the new creation which makes of us a new creature and which is called adoption, the rebirth in Jesus Christ. It was necessary to maintain later on that human freedom was by no means diminished accordingly nor, even less, annihilated. Thus St. Leo IX, in his *Symbolum fidei* of 1053, teaches: *Gratiam Dei praevenire et subsequi hominem credo et profiteor, ita tamen, ut liberum arbitrium rationali creaturae non denegem*[1]. And later, in a text which Maurice Blondel loved to

1 *Denz*, 348.

quote, St. Bernard would write, in his treatise *De gratia et libero arbitrio*:

Ipsa (gratia) liberum excitat arbitrium, cum seminat cogitatum, sanat, cum immutat affectum; roborat, ut perducat ad actum; servat, ne sentiat defectum. Sic autem ista cum libero arbitrio operatur, ut tantum illud in primo praeveniat, in caeteris comitetur; ad hoc utique praeveniens, ut jam sibi deinceps cooperetur. Ita tamen quod a sola gratia coeptum est, pariter ab utroque perficitur: ut mixtim, non singillatim; non vicissim, per singulos profectus operentur. Non partim gratia, partim liberum arbitrium, sed totum singula opere individuo peragunt. Totum quidem hoc, et totum illa; sed ut totum in illo, sic totum ex illa[2].

"For we are God's coadjutors", as St. Paul had already written. The operation of grace in us does not transform us without ourselves; it does not work upon a passive and inert being. It gives birth to a liberty; it regenerates that which was feeble; it creates powers of action and of thought. It makes of us creators. It does not divinize us without our co-operation.

We know that at the heart of this problem of the co-operation of man in the divinizing action of God in him, is located, amongst other things, the opposition between Catholic theology and the theology born of the Reforma-

2 *Tract de Gratia et Libero Arbitrio*, ch. xiv, 47.

tion. It is the whole question of human nature which is involved.

Let us note here the profound, ontological homogeneity between the theological theses defined by the Church in different centuries. In opposition to the Monophysites and the Monothelites, the Church defined, at the Council of Chalcedon and at the Third Council of Constantinople, that in the unique person of Christ it is proper to distinguish two natures, the divine and the human, and consequently two wills, without conflict, freely conjoined. The human will is obedient to the divine will and thus co-operates in the work of our divinization. We see how the doctrine of co-operation, formulated by St. Paul and defined at the Council of Trent, is intrinsically linked with traditional Christology. In Christ Jesus, human nature co-operates freely in the work of divinization. Correlatively, in an ontological liaison with this divinization, the whole of humanity has the duty of co-operating in the work of sanctification. In the unique person of Christ, the assimilation of human nature does not take place without a co-operation of this human nature; it does not remain passive. Moreover, in the work of our sanctification, man is not justified from without, in a merely juridical fashion and without his co-operation.

The Council of Trent defined that justification is not an extrinsic imputation, a juridical decision which forgives us our sins, but rather, it is a fundamental re-creation, a sanctification which renews our being, a regeneration which makes of us a new creature, in the words of St. Paul.

Justification itself . . . consists not merely in the remission of sins but also in the sanctification and renewal of the interior man by the voluntary reception of grace and gifts, whence a man becomes just instead of unjust and a friend instead of an enemy, in order to be an heir "according to the hope of eternal life"[3].

The sole formal cause (of justification) is the justice of God, not that by which he is himself just, but that by which he makes us just, that namely of what he bestows upon us by which we are renewed in the spirit of our mind, and we are not reputed to be but are truly named and are just, receiving in us justice, each his own according to the measure which the Holy Spirit "divides to every one as he wills" (1 Cor. 12:11) and according to each one's own disposition and co-operation[4].

The canons of the Council of Trent concerning justification formally condemn the doctrines which deny this co-operation of man in the work of his sanctification, and which regard human nature damaged to such an extent by sin that human freedom no longer exists:

If anyone says that the free will of man moved and stimulated by God in no wise co-operates in assenting to God who rouses and calls, by which he disposes and prepares himself to obtain the grace of justification, and that he cannot refuse his consent if he

3 *Denz*, 799.
4 *ibid*.

wishes, but like an inanimate thing does nothing whatsoever and plays a purely passive part, let him be anathema[5].

If anyone says that after the sin of Adam the free will of man was lost and done away with, or that it is a thing which has a name only or rather that it is a name without a reality, or finally a fiction brought into the Church by Satan, let him be anathema[6].

We see therefore that the difference between Catholic theology and the Reformed theology or theologies lies also on a metaphysical plane, at a metaphysical level. Perhaps indeed it is at the metaphysical level that decisions are taken which will intervene on the theological plane.

"Original sin", according to Catholic theology, has not altered human nature in its substance (or in its essence); it remains as it was on emerging from the hands of God. It remains beautiful, and excellent. What is altered is not human nature itself, but the relations, properly supernatural, between God and man. The difference between Catholic theology and the Reformed theologies becomes evident without a doubt on this point. For the theologies barn of the Reformation "original sin" has altered human nature itself. Human nature is radically corrupted, vitiated, denatured, reduced to impotence, as much from the point of view of understanding as from the point of view of action and freedom.

In an article in the *Summa Theologica* devoted to the

5 *Denz,* 814.
6 *Denz,* 815.

condition of man before sin, St. Thomas Aquinas poses the question of whether, in the state of innocence, there already was generation from physical union of man and woman. St. Thomas answers:

> Certain ancient Doctors, considering the fetid character of concupiscence which is found in carnal union in the present condition, have laid down that in the state of innocence there was not generation by coitus. Whence Gregory of Nyssa says in his book *On the creation of man* (Chapt. 17) that in Paradise the multiplication of the human race would have been otherwise, after the manner in which angels are multiplied, without copulation, by the operation of the power of God. And he says that God, before sin, made male and female having regard to the manner of generation which was to be after sin, of which God was prescient.
>
> But this is not reasonable. *Sed hoc non dicitur rationabiliter.* In fact, *the things which are natural to man are neither taken away from nor given to man in consequence of sin. Ea enim quae sunt naturalia homini, neque subtrahuntur neque dantur homini per peccatum*[7].

This principle holds true for the Catholic theology of original sin and, with regard to our subject, for the Catholic doctrine of human nature with respect to original sin.

7 *Summa Theologica*, Iᵃ q. xcviii, art. 2.

Today our contemporaries are embarrassed by a particular representation of the doctrine of original sin which they ascribe to Christian (Catholic) dogma, which in fact not only does not correspond to the thought of the Church in this field but strongly resembles theses which the Church has never ceased to reject in connection with the doctrine of original sin. This misunderstanding has often been pointed out[8].

I do not have to supply here the Catholic theology of original sin. A statement of it will be found in all the classical treatises on dogma. Moreover, it is easier to determine what original sin is not (from the conciliar definitions which dismiss erroneous theses), than what it is. According to Catholic theology, what is here and now certain is that existing human nature, as we know it by concrete experience, is indeed that which emerged from the hands of the Creator. It is not a new nature, born of sin, caused by sin. Nothing has been taken away from the nature originally created; nothing has been added. According to the Gnostic myths and Plotinus, something was added in consequence to a primitive fault—corporality, individuality. According to certain theological representations not accepted by the Church, something has been taken away from human nature as originally created. According to Catholic theology, sin has not altered human nature fundamentally, as it was created. Sin has altered the relations between God and man, not the essence of man. Our present nature is not a

---

8 *Cf.* for example, J.-V. Bainvel, *Nature et surnaturel*, Paris, 1920; A. Verriele, *Le surnaturel en nous et le péché originel*, Paris, 1932; E. Masure, *L'Humanisme chrétien*, Paris, 1937.

perverted or changed nature. Our present nature remains
the human nature created by God. The Catholic doctrine
of original sin establishes itself on another plane, that of the
supernatural relations between man and his Creator. What
is changed by sin is the holiness of man. This is what the
Old Testament and, following it, St. Paul call "justice".

Without entering into a properly theological statement
on original sin—which is not my province—I can nevertheless offer some very simple observations which will permit us to come to the Christian dogma of original sin, starting from common experience.

Man is responsible for the evil that he commits. Human
evil is not inevitable, either as a necessity of nature, imposed by creation, or as an external necessity, an astral or
divine fate. Sin does not proceed in a necessary manner
from human nature. It proceeds from human freedom. One
can therefore legitimately conceive, at least as a hypothesis,
of a time before sin and a time after. Since sin is not necessary, one can imagine (without contradiction, and at least
as a hypothesis, as the mathematicians do) a state of innocence and of holiness, anterior to sin. Again, human nature
is not, by creation, evil. Fundamentally, evil is the work of
man; it is created by man; it is the fruit of the thoughts of
his heart. Augustine fought against Manicheism partly in
order to rescue this responsibility within man.

It is not by creation or construction of human nature
that man is unhappy. By creation, by nature, man is made
for happiness. If man has lost this happiness, it is his own
responsibility; that is something we see proved again today.
Humanity is unhappy because it destroys, oppresses, ex-

ploits, and humilitates itself. Humanity, today as ever, makes its own misfortune. Neither war, nor exploitation, nor oppression, nor torture, nor the pauperization of man by man is the result of a necessity of nature. They are the work of human freedom.

The child is not born with the life of God, to which he is called, in him. According to Christianity, man is invited to a destiny properly supernatural—participation in the life of God, divinization. The child is not born in the fulness of the possession of this supernatural and divine life. It must be brought to him. The happy tidings must be announced to him. He must enter into the Church. He must consent to the call of grace in him. He must, in the words of St. Paul and of the Fourth Gospel, consent to a new birth, which will make him a new creature. This birth is spiritual, supernatural. The living soul is made into a vivifying spirit. Therefore, in actual fact, a disparity exists between what the child is at birth and what it is called to become. He is born "deprived of the divine life".

This divine life, as its name indicates, comes from God. Grace is first. It is the grace of God which will make this child, born with a soul, into a new, spiritual creature.

The child is born in fact, into a world of sin, into a criminal world. It inherits biological determinisms, taints, on the physiological and psychological plane. These taints can themselves be the consequence of positive faults committed by ancestors. But the child is going to inherit also, and especially by the education which he is going to receive from his environment, a set of ready-made ideas, a system of judgments, a scale of values which, as often as not, he will not be able to question or criticize. This system of values, in the aggregate of nations, in large part is criminal. It is the reflection of a criminal world in which man oppresses, massacres, tortures, humiliates, and exploits his brother. The child enters into an organized world, on the political, economic, mental, mythological, psychological, and other planes. And the structure of this world is penetrated and informed by sin. The child is not born in Paradise. It is born in a criminal humanity. In order to have access to justice, to sanctity, the child, as it grows up, will have to make a personal act of judgment, of refusal, of choice. It will have to make a personal act of opposition to the values of its tribe, of its caste, of its nation or of its race, and of its social class, in order to attain justice. To a certain extent it will have to leave its tribe, its nation, its caste, its class, its race, as Abraham the father of the faithful did, he who left Ur of the Chaldees to go into a country that he did not know. Holiness begins with a breach. Nothing can dispense the child from this personal act of breaking with "the world". In order to enter into Christianity, the child will have to choose between the values of the world, the values of its tribe, its nation or its social class, and the values of the Gospel. It must renew its scale of values. It must, as it were, be born anew, from the spiritual point of view; it must become a new creature. Tertullian said one is not born a Christian. One becomes a Christian. The access to Christianity represents a new birth. One can then legitimately distinguish between the state which precedes this new birth and the state which follows it. The state which precedes this new birth is the state which the Church calls "original sin".

The Church did not imply in its solemn definitions, however, that the nature of man might be radically and ontologically perverted by original sin. On the contrary, she has firmly dismissed the doctrines of those who invented a human nature whose mythical origins describe the present fall and abasement after the manner of the Gnostics. She has maintained that in his present condition man, as much from the point of view of freedom as from the point of view of understanding, remains *capax Dei*. Later, we shall meet again the problems concerned with human reason. It is in these two domains that Catholic theology is fundamentally opposed to the theology or theologies born of the Reformation. Thus the fundamental differences appear on the metaphysical plane. They result from a divergent understanding of "original sin".

CHAPTER SIX

The Supernatural Destiny of Man

According to Christianity, creation does not have an end in itself. Creation, as we have seen, is not a necessary procession of the multiple from the one, nor is it a fall. It is a gift, an expression of the absolute *agape*. But this creation is not, if one may so put it, merely centrifugal. It does not consist merely in raising up, contriving, and placing in existence innumerable beings, for their good and their joy. In fact, according to Christianity, the term of creation is a marriage, a real union, without confusion of natures, of created persons and uncreated. In order that there may be real union the created beings must attain this level of the person. In order that the union of a created being and an uncreated God may be possible, the created being must attain a specific level. It must be *capax Dei*. It must be pre-adapted to this union. And this pre-adaptation is the work of creation.

In creation then, there is, there will be, according to Christianity, a real union, without confusion, of the human and divine natures. We shall be, according to an epistle attributed to Peter, *consortes divinae naturae*, participators in the divine nature. The doctrine of divinization completes the doctrine of creation. It provides its key and meaning. There is therefore a movement which one may call centripetal, resolving at the same time whatever spatial character this image may have. We have not indeed come out of the divine nature or essence, because we are not made of the divine substance, and therefore we do not have to return to it. But creation places us in some manner outside of God, ontologically distinct from God. The call to divinization is an invitation to the union which puts God in all. We are not outside of God as an object is outside of a determined space. In God we are and live and move, by creation. But the union which is proposed to us is not a union of fact, laid down by creation; it is a union of grace, a loving union in which we have to consent.

The distinction between nature and the supernatural thus appears to be almost inevitable, when the distinction between creation and divinization is understood. We are not divinized as soon as we are created. Our divinization is not a state of fact, established from all eternity. Our divinization is a process, a genesis, in which grace is primary, but in which we have to co-operate freely. Man cannot be divinized automatically, because God cannot create a god without the consent of the creature—a god in spite of himself. Divinization cannot be given in such a way that the divinized being receives it in a passive manner. Therefore, a certain distinction of time and moments appears to be inevitable. There is the time of creation, by which we are composed and made beings. And then there is the time or period of divinization, a period in which we consent to and co-operate with the invitation which is freely proposed to us. (In infant baptism, this consent comes through the persons

of the godparents, who act as spokesmen for the infant.)
One cannot imagine automatic and direct divinization
without the suppression of what is precisely in question—
freedom, by which we are created in the image and likeness
of God. The time of creation is not a superfluous time; it is
the time necessary for created man to serve his apprenticeship to the godhead, an apprenticeship from which nothing
can dispense him. A god is not created in spite of himself.
Human dignity imposes this duration of probation and
growth, this noviciate in preparation for the eternal union.
The fundamental originality of Christian anthropology is
therefore distinguished as follows.

According to Brahminic theosophy, Orphism, Platonism, Neoplatonism, and the Gnosis, the soul is a particle
of the divine substance; it is naturally divine, but it has for-
gotten its divine essence, fallen into an evil body, and become alienated in materiality and corporality. Individuation
is a fall; it results from embodiedness. Salvation for the soul
consists in liberating itself from the bonds of the body by
ascesis and initiation, returning to the dear fatherland from
which it proceeds, retracing the path which it traversed in
its fall, undoing what the procession has done, or repairing
what it has undone. Thus the soul will recognize that it is of
divine essence, that it is *pars divinae substantiae*, that individuation, individual existence, is an illusion and that, as
the Upanishads and Plotinus say, we are all one.

Christian thought has rejected this myth. The soul is not
of divine essence; it is ontologically distinct from the absolute, created by him and did not emanate from him. It is
not a particle of the divine substance. It is, on the other
hand, called, invited, by grace, to participate in the life of

God, to share in the nature of God, *consortes naturae divinae*. It is called to adoption, to divinization. Therefore, divinization is, at the term of creation, the work of grace, with which human freedom co-operates. There is no question of natural and original divinity of the soul, but divinization which is ultimate and final, supernatural, of man, in Christ, by the spirit.

One sees that the difference between Christian and pagan anthropologies is fundamental, radical, and insurmountable.

Christian metaphysics is characterized by an opening to the supernatural. The Christian vision of things is not monist. We are not particles of the single substance of the whole. Therefore, according to Christian metaphysics, relationships of dialogue exist between the uncreated being and the created beings. The absolute enters into a personal relationship with man, in particular, within the outline of a new humanity—the people of God—through the instrumentality of the *nabi*. Even within man, by the immanence of the Spirit of God, a personal relationship establishes itself between the absolute and the created persons. These relations between the creative absolute and the created persons are free. They constitute a new gift, a new grace. They are not inscribed in created nature in a necessary manner. They proceed from the freedom of God. We say that they are supernatural. They constitute the outline, the pledge, and the efficacious means of a radical transformation, of a real divinization.

According to a metaphysic such as Spinozism, for example, the relations between the human soul and God are not relations of dialogue since the human soul is in fact consubstantial with God. The relations between the human soul and the substance are the relations which exist between a modality of the divine substance and the substance itself. They stay within the identity of the substance or of the divine nature. In a metaphysic of this kind, therefore, there is no properly supernatural element for man. All is nature. All is derived from the same nature.

The originality of the Christian metaphysic, in contrast to metaphysics of this kind, lies in the possibility of a supernatural dimension, a possibility which results from the very structure of that metaphysic; it is a metaphysic of creation. At the same time, it may be held that this is no longer metaphysics; we are now in the realm of theology. With the doctrine of divinization, we are at the heart of Christian theology; we are in the midst of the revealed supernatural. This must be admitted. It must also be noted that the philosophies most traditionally listed in the history of metaphysical thought—those of Plato, Plotinus, Spinoza, Leibniz, Fichte, Schelling, Hegel, and many others—also comprise a doctrine of pantheistic divinization. The soul is naturally, eternally, of divine nature. It has fallen into a world which banishes it, into a body which emprisons it; it is alienated and exiled in nature, far from the divine essence. But it will return to the divine essence, to its truth. The process is cyclic; it is natural, in the sense that it does not appeal to a supernatural gift, to a grace. This cycle is regarded as being fully entitled to form part of what is called metaphysics. The Platonic, Plotinian, Spinozan, or Hegelian doctrine of the divine, of the soul, of its origin or destiny, is not refused a place in our histories of philosophy. Why should Christian doctrine on the same subjects be dismissed from the field of metaphysics? Is it because it is not pantheistic? But should pantheism be *a priori* identifiable with the rational and the philosophic? That is what certain authors seem to think, at least implicitly—those authors who welcome into their histories of philosophy the myths of Plato, Plotinus, Schelling, and many others, but cast Christianity into exterior darkness because it recognizes the supernatural, because it recognizes a doctrine of creation which distinguishes the absolute from the world, and thinks it perceives relationships of freedom between the absolute and created man.

If the Brahminic, Platonic, Plotinian, and Spinozan philosophies and the great systems of German idealism are admitted into metaphysical thought, there is no reason not to receive Christianity as well, a metaphysic in the same right as the others. If one specifies, in a history of metaphysics, the wish to retain only the positive part, that which is dependent on pure reason, one must begin by ruling out many of the most fundamental specluations and theses of the philosophies of Plato, Aristotle, Plotinus, Spinoza, Fichte, Hegel, Schelling, and others. One can submit Christianity to the same treatment and discuss whether the Christian supernatural is irrational, in the same way as the Orphic mythology, which carries through from Plato to Schelling. Then one would finally come up against the problem posed by Maurice Blondel as long ago as 1893: to what extent can the Christian supernatural be dismissed from the field of rational reflection? In concrete reality, to what extent does it not comprise marks discoverable by positive and scientific reason? To what extent is a "separate" philosophy legitimate? To what extent is empirical and concrete reality not pre-adapted, by construction, by creation, to this supernatural end to which Christianity points? To what extent, therefore, is this fundamental structure of the real, at its different levels, perhaps capable of showing forth the immanent operation of the supernatural which in fact fashions this creation? Can the Babylonian or Orphic mythologies and the Christian supernatural both be nonsuited? This is what must be philosophically investigated. Pending the completion of such an examination, Christian metaphysics has its legitimate and rightful place among the other existing metaphysics in the world.

What is taught by the whole of the Old Testament, the New Testament, the Fathers, and the unanimous Christian tradition is that man is called to a supernatural destiny. Thus, from the Old Testament onwards, we establish the fact that the absolute enters into a relationship of dialogue with man, specifically with chosen men, the *nabis*—Abraham, Moses, Elias, Amos, and others. The prophets of Israel conceive human history as destined to reach completion in a union of God and his universal people. From that time on there is knowledge of a filiation, of an adoption. In the New Testament the whole evangelical message takes its direction from this invitation to the divine union, this call to a new birth which will make of us sons of God. The very theology of Christ, Christology, points essentially to this supernatural destiny proposed for man. This divinization is possible since in Christ human nature is assumed, elevated, and divinized, united without separation or confusion with the divine nature. That is why Christ is the "head" of the body which is the Church, the germinal cell of this new humanity, inhabited by God, consecrated, divinized, the temple of the living God, the spouse of Christ. The very doctrine of the Eucharist is the efficacious sign of this consecration and divinization. It is in St. Paul that we find the most positive formulations of this marriage of Christ and the Church, of which human marriage is the sign, a union by which God is all in all. The deification of humanity is begun in Christ. It is in Christ that we are created new, born anew; it is in him that we become participators in the divine nature, *consortes divinae naturae*. Such is the key to Christianity. The Rabbis regard the *Canticle of Canticles* as the central book of the Scriptures. So also do the Christian mystics. The marriage spoken of in the *Canticle of Canticles* is indeed the great *mysterium*, which alone gives meaning to the entire creation.

The doctrine of divinization has been developed, clarified, and annotated by the Fathers, Irenaeus, Gregory Nazianzen, Basil of Caesarea, Cyril of Alexandria, Athanasius of Alexandria, Chrysostom, and, on the Latin side, Augustine. Monographs have been devoted to the doctrine of divinization in the Fathers. We do not need to cite here the numerous texts which attest to its continuity.

If we refer to the other end of the Church's history, if we move forward to a nearly contemporary epoch, we find in the constitution *De Fide* of the Vatican Council a formulation of the supernatural end of man:

God, out of his infinite goodness, ordained man to a supernatural end, that is to say to a sharing in the divine estate, which altogether transcends the intelligence of the human mind[9].

One of the three editors of the constitution *De Fide*, Cardinal Dechamps, writes in the same way:

It is in the participation in the knowledge, love and life of God himself by the means which he has willed, by the incarnation, by revelation, by grace, by the sacraments, by the virtues full of grace in this world and by the light of glory and the beatific vision in the other, it is in this participation in the divine life that the supernatural destiny of man and the supernatural order itself consist, that is to say the supernatural in its inner, full, permanent condition, the supernatural in its strict sense[10].

Thus the doctrine of the supernaturalization, of the divinization of created humanity is certainly an established and well-defined doctrine, constitutive of Christianity. The entire Christian metaphysic is in fact directed and pre-adapted, by construction, to this supernatural dimension. The whole of creation, according to Christianity, is directed and pre-adapted to its supernatural end. It is then permissible for the philosopher to study, by the methods

9 *Denz*, 1786.
10 Cardinal Dechamps, Oeuvres, XVII, 173: quoted by Henri de Lubac, *Surnaturel*, Paris, 1946, 422.

proper to him, this pre-adaptation of created being to its supernatural end. The supernatural comes not only from without, in a wholly extrinsic and arbitrary manner. It is prepared and called for from within. The supernatural does not add itself to created nature as an arbitrary and factitious supplement. In fact, by creation, the Creator disposes the created being interiorly to that supernatural end which is freely and graciously proposed to him, and to which he is invited to freely respond. There is no exigency on the part of the created being; just as creation is a gift, so also is the supernatural end which is proposed. But in the created and personal being there is a disposition, an orientation, and a desire which are the work of creation and grace in us, and which the philosopher may study with the rational means at his disposal. This pre-adaptation of created being to its supernatural end is visible, ascertainable, verifiable, triable, and analyzable. Concrete, human reality, affected by the supernatural, calls for the end which is intended for it.

We distinguish in this connection two orders of questions. On the one hand, created nature, by construction, by creation, is pre-adapted to its supernatural end, so that it is permissible to discern in nature a *desiderium naturale sed inefficax videndi Deum*. This is a debatable but free question. On the other hand, in concrete, human reality, grace and the supernatural, in actual fact, work upon the living man. One can then discern in concrete man, in his action, in his will, in his thought, in his very being, traces of the supernatural which dispose man to that end to which he is called. It will be seen that the two planes are different.

We know that controversies and polemics have developed about these problems, which it is not my business to enumerate in the present sketch. The work of Maurice Blondel, and of Fr. Laberthonnière in a perceptibly different fashion, have dealt with a properly philosophical analysis of what bore witness in concrete, human reality to this work of the supernatural in us, to this pre-adaptation of the created being to its supernatural end, to the whole movement by which the created being disposes and orientates itself, in its action, thought, and being, towards this unique end[11].

The question whether Christian metaphysics can or cannot, should or should not find a place in a history of philosophy revolves around the question of the supernatural. If the Christian supernatural, taught by revelation and by the Church, finds in man no rationally discoverable correspondence, no touchstone of anticipation, no petition, and presents itself as a superfluous supplement falling on a complete, contented, fulfilled, self-satisfied human nature, then philosophy can question the rational value of this idea of the supernatural for which experience offers no foundation. Then it will be possible to legitimately attempt to establish a separate philosophy. Christianity will remain a metaphysic, in the same right as the metaphysics of Brahminism, Platonism, Neoplatonism, and Spinozism—but it will not have a rational title. It will be dependent on a gratuitous choice, or philosophically arbitrary preference, instead of on philosophy.

11 Concerning the whole problem of the supernatural, *cf*. Verriele, *op. cit.*; E. Masure, *op. cit.*; H. de Lubac, *op. cit.*

But if, on the contrary, the Christian supernatural finds in creation some preparations, pre-adaptation, touchstones of anticipation, predispositions, which are rationally analyzable and discoverable, then one can no longer say that the Christian supernatural is arbitrary, superfluous, and useless. It will appear required by experimental reality itself, inserted in concrete, human reality in a way which is not factitious but congenital. Any separate philosophy then is condemned, because nature does not exist in a separate manner.

CHAPTER SEVEN

The Doctrine
of Cognition—
Christianity and Reason

CHRISTIANITY COMPRISES a doctrine of reason which is bound up in its ontology and metaphysics. According to Christianity, creation, which is not consubstantial with God, does manifest God. It is the expression of his thought, of his magnificence, as the poem is the expression of the thought of the poet. Man is part of this creation. He is a creature, and from this creation he can gropingly regain creative thought. God, says St. Paul (*Acts* 14:15), "in times past suffered all nations to walk in their own ways. Nevertheless he left not himself without testimony, doing good from heaven, giving rains and fruitful seasons, filling our hearts with food and gladness". There exists, therefore, a natural knowledge of God, from creation, for all men at all times. This is what Paul expounds in his *Epistle to the Romans* (1:18 *et seq.*). The good things of creation, the gifts of creation are the expression of the rich, creative generosity. The beauty of creation and the delight of the children of men bear witness that creation is a boon for man. Fruit is provided for man's hunger. Woman is a blessing for man, as man is a blessing for woman. In the economy of creation itself, the human intelligence, apart from any supernatural manifestation of God to man, can discern the divinity and power of him who acts from the beginning of time. It is an established doctrine in the biblical and orthodox Christian tradition that creation shows forth the hidden God and leads to knowledge of him.

This constant doctrine of the biblical and Christian tradition can be rejected, and has in fact been rejected for several reasons.

1. In certain dualist systems, such as that of Marcion, the creator of this sensible and visible world is not the good god. The good god is a "strange god" who will come to save the human soul which he has not created. Sensible and visible creation cannot then manifest the "unknown god", the "strange god", the "good god", since it is not his work. There is no connection, no ontological relationship between creation and the good god. Creation is the work of another god, who is the evil principle. To say that creation in no way shows forth God the creator is to introduce an ontological breach, a separation, between God and his work. There is indeed no consubstantiality between God and his work; the created is in no way part of the divine substance, or a modality of the absolute. But there is nevertheless a relationship and a manifestation, as, according to John (1:1), the entire creation was made "in the logos of God".

2. A second reason which has led certain theological schools to reject the possibility of the natural knowledge of God is a marked pessimism about human nature and human knowledge. Human nature is so vitiated and corrupted, in virtue of original sin, that the human intelligence

is incapable of attaining, by its own powers, knowledge of God. As we have noted, this conception of original sin is foreign to Catholic theology, which maintains that human nature, constituted by creation, is fundamentally unaltered by sin. Nothing is added or taken away because of sin, writes St. Thomas Aquinas in an earlier quoted text.

In both cases, at the source of the denial of a natural knowledge of God, we find a pronounced pessimism regarding creation, be it original or actual. Catholic tradition does not share this pessimism[1].

Catholic theology, or more precisely the thought of the Church, defined at the Vatican Council that human reason can, from creation, raise itself to the knowledge of him who is the creator of all. This definition does not mean that all men in fact do thus have access to the knowledge of the living God, but that access is possible, and the Church was bent on defining this possibility in regard to the doctrine of human nature and, ultimately, in regard to the doctrine of creation. It is the very dignity of the thinking creature which is in question. If man were truly incapable, by nature, of having access to a natural knowledge of God through creation, faith would be a purely extrinsic intrusion, without rational justification in the heart of the believ-

1 We refer the reader, on this question of the natural knowledge of God, and more precisely, on the conflict between Catholic and Protestant theology on this subject, to Henri Bouillard, *Karl Barth*, Paris, 1957, Vol. III, *et. al.* This volume contains chapters treating the possibility of the knowledge of God and the problem of natural theology. Unquestionably, this book is one of the most penetrating, philosophical analyses of the difference, at the philosophical level, between Catholic and Protestant theologies.

ing subject. Here, we meet again the same doctrine of human passivity which previously characterized the Lutheran doctrine of justification, human reason imputed from without but not transformed from within. Catholic theology, for its part, was bent on maintaining the possibility of a co-operation of man in the work of justification and sanctification, and at the same time, in the act of faith[2]. Faith is not a passion endured. It is not the consequence of a breaking in, of a violent supernatural intrusion upon us. Faith is a free[3] and reasonable[4] act, grounded in supernatural[5] reason, but with the co-operation of all the natural powers of man. Faith, both supernatural and rational, is the joint work of the grace of God and human freedom, as is justification. Faith is not, to use Kierkegaard's phrase, a "qualitative leap into the absurd". Such a leap is not required. Faith is grounded, in reason, in experience, in the nature of things, in history, in creation, in sacred history, in the history of the Church. The worship asked of us is a reasonable worship, which completes rather than abolishes nature. Faith is not a harrowing and tragic leap, but a pleasant and peaceful act, in which our eyes perceive the natural and supernatural evidence of God.

The doctrine by which human reason can, even apart from historial revelation, have access to the knowledge of God remains unchanged in the Church since St. Paul. It is

2 *Denz*, 1791.
3 *Denz*, 1814.
4 *Denz*, 1790.
5 *Denz*, 1789.

defined, in contrast to those who would deny it, in the Constitution *De Fide* of the Vatican Council:

The same Holy Mother Church holds and teaches that by the natural light of human reason, God, the beginning and end of all things can be certainly known from created things; "for the invisible things of him, from the creation of the world, are clearly seen, being understood by the things that are made" (*Rom.* 1: 20); that nevertheless is pleased the wisdom and goodness of God to reveal himself and the eternal decrees of his will to the human race in another, supernatural way; as the Apostle says, "God, who, at sundry times and in divers manners, spoke in times past to the fathers by the prophets, last of all, in these days hath spoken to us by his Son" (*Hebrews* 1: 1 *et seq.*)[6].

With this chapter of the Constitution *De Fide* is connected the canon which condemns the contrary thesis:

If anyone says that the one and true God, our Creator and Lord, cannot be certainly known, through those things which are made, by the natural light of human reason, let him be anathema[7].

Once more, the Fathers of the Vatican Council did not intend to define that, within the Church, men have access

6 *Denz*, 1785.
7 *Denz*, 1806.

to the knowledge of God by this philosophical and rational path, nor that philosophers may arrive at a knowledge of God, outside the Church, by a metaphysical analysis of this kind. What they defined is that human reason is capable of this knowledge. What we have here, then, is a definition concerning human nature. Human nature, human reason, by constitution, is capable of having access to the knowledge of the creative absolute; this is contrary, for example, to the critique of Kant. Human reason is not damaged, by virtue of sin, to the extent that it is no longer able to exert itself normally, and to attain this knowledge; the Lutheran doctrine is here opposed.

This traditional doctrine is formulated among many others, by one of the writers of the Constitution *De Fide*, Cardinal Dechamps, who throughout his work has defended the reality, powers, and legitimate rights of reason, in order "to dispel the prejudice because of which it is thought, through half-knowledge, that reason has absolutely nothing to see in dogma"[8]. As he rightly remarked, "It would have been unworthy of God to speak to the world a word which would have no meaning for man, even here below"[9]. Again, if man was not a knowing subject, pre-adapted by nature, by construction, by creation to this knowledge of God, the manifestation of God to man would have been a rape of conscience, an unjustifiable and arbitrary intrusion. Before the Council, Cardinal Dechamps developed the doctrine of reason which is a prerequisite, a presupposition, to the Christian theology of faith:

8 Dechamps, *op. cit.*, XVI, 54.
9 Dechamps, *op. cit.*, I, 8.

The infallibility of the teaching Church, in the pres-
ervation of the deposit of faith, is not the only infallibility which may be misunderstood in our time, and
the defence of which must be undertaken by the
Council. The supernatural infallibility which faith-
fully watches over the world according to the prom-
ises of Jesus Christ, the divinely revealed truth presupposes the natural infallibility or certain authority
of the reason in those matters which are within its
competence . . .

It is the reason . . . which calls to revelation and it
is to the reason that revelation addresses itself. It is to
the reason that God speaks, it is of the reason he asks
faith, and he does not ask it of it until after he has
made it see that it is indeed he who speaks. The reason
which asks for the testimony of God concerning the
realities of the future life does not then cleave to this
testimony with the supernatural certainty of faith until
it has seen with its own eyes—verified, that is to say,
by its own light and with the natural certainty which is
its own—the divine fact of revelation.

Later, Cardinal Dechamps calls to mind "the infallible
natural certainty with which the reason grasps the infallible
supernatural certainty of faith"[10].

Therefore, Catholic, Christian thought has explicitly
made clear that it comprises a doctrine of reason which is

10 Dechamps, *l'Infaillibilité et le concile général*, May 29, 1869, in
E. Cecconi, *Histoire du concile du Vatican*, vol. IV, Fr. trans.,
1887.

not any doctrine whatsoever, and which is bound up with the whole of the Christian metaphysic. In this connection Christian thought has had to fight on two fronts, as was frequently the case with other problems. In opposition to an illegitimate undervaluing of reason, Catholic thought has maintained its excellence. Contrary to an epistemology which, in fact, depends on a pantheistic ontology, Catholic thought has maintained that the human reason is created, and that it does not contain an immediate and congenital, natural knowledge of the absolute. In fact, what the theologians call "rationalism" is the doctrine according to which human reason is the measure of everything. The human reason is created. It derives its worth, its power, and its stability from this act of creation. To disparage reason and scorn its power is to disparage and scorn this creation, which the Church has always refused to do. The human reason is powerful in its order. So fideism is condemned.

But human reason is not divine reason. The human soul is not *pars divinae substantiae*. Human reason does not know God by a natural or connatural intuition. The Church has rejected ontologism, which rests on the presupposition that a part of human reason is divine.

If the human reason is not uncreated, a relationship of dialogue is possible between it and the absolute, from which it is distinct. Human reason is not the measure of the intelligible, since it is not the divine reason, or a particle of the absolute reason. Here "rationalism", for which the human reason is the measure of what is absolutely possible, is condemned.

The Catholic doctrine of reason therefore sets itself in

opposition to fideism, which undervalues the human reason, to ontologism, which regards the human reason as capable of knowing the absolute naturally, and to "rationalism", which denies that truth may be more immense than that which the human reason can comprehend in its natural state as creature.

What precisely is meant, in the language of Catholic theologians, by the term "rationalism"?

The term today has several meanings, which are essential to distinguish.

1. What is commonly understood today by the word "rationalism" is a doctrine or tendency which is directed toward maintaining the rights of reason, which refuses to sacrifice the legitimate requirements of reason to acceptance of obscure and equivocal criteria such as undefinable intuition, tradition or traditions, initiation or gnoses, feeling, subjective impression, and so forth. "Rationalism" thus understood is opposed to irrationalism in all its forms—fideism, occultism, esotericism, romanticism, and other forms.

Let us say at once that this claim on behalf of reason is entirely legitimate and that if one understands "rationalism" in this sense, Catholic Christianity is "rationalist". As we will see, Catholic tradition has constantly upheld the rights and powers of the reason against every disparagement of it. The demands of rationality are legitimate, natural, and healthy. The "rationalism" of modern science is valid and good.

2. But in the ecclesiastical documents, and, in particular, in the prologue to the Constitution *Dei Filius* of the

Vatican Council, the term "rationalism" is not understood in this sense. In this text, and more often than not in the thought of Catholic theologians, the term "rationalism" is neither opposed to fideism nor to irrationalism; they do not have this opposition in mind when they speak of "rationalism". The theologians, following the Vatican Council, mean by "rationalism" the doctrine according to which the natural, human reason is self-sufficient, is the norm and criterion of the real and the possible. The Catholic theologians deny this doctrine. The human reason is created, is excellent in its order, and is powerful in its order, but it is not the absolute criterion and the norm of all being, known and unknown. In other words, being extends widely beyond what is known and knowable by the reason. The supreme norm, the absolute criterion to which the reason must be referred, is uncreated truth. If it pleases God to make truths known to man which man was incapable of discovering by his natural powers in his present condition, the human reason would have no right to refuse this gift of a properly supernatural knowledge. "Rationalism", understood in this sense, is the pretension to self-sufficiency. Man is not the measure of all things. It is God who is the measure of all things. The existence of God is knowable with certainty by natural reason; but God can communicate truths to man, which man, by his reason alone, is incapable of discovering. "Rationalism" then, understood in this sense, consists in denying the Christian supernatural, the possibility of the supernatural, the possibility of a free manifestation of God to man.

From the philosophical point of view, which is our position here, it must be said that this claim to deny the possibility of a revelation, the possibility of the supernatural is exorbitant. The human reason has no right to refuse something which it does not know yet, to reject *a priori* this gracious manifestation of God to man. It is a paralogism to deny the possibility of the supernatural in the name of nature. From the rational point of view, nothing justifies this denial *a priori*, just as nothing would justify the blind acceptance of this manifestation of God to man without rational criteria. As Bergson has shown in masterly analyses, the possible is not known until afterwards. It cannot be determined before. We will know afterwards what is and is not possible. The possible does not precede the actual. The actual does not conform to a possible, determined from all previous eternity. What is, is evidently possible. What will be, is evidently possible. What will have been, will have been possible. If it pleases God to show himself to man, then it is in actual fact possible. Human reason has no jurisdiction over the possible.

"Rationalism", in the thought of Catholic theologians, is therefore almost a synonym for "naturalism"—the claim to regard nature as the sole existence, and therefore as the sole criterion of the possible and the actual. Naturalism is then either an atheism or a pantheism, since it only recognizes existence from its empirically established nature, *natura sive Deus*. In fact, the difference between pantheism and atheism is perhaps only nominal. "Atheism is only an inverted pantheism", said Feuerbach.

We see how the Christian doctrine of reason is connected with Christian ontology.

Then there has been born and all too widely
diffused throughout the world that doctrine of rationalism or naturalism which, opposing in every way the
Christian religion inasmuch as it is a supernatural in-
stitution, strives with the greatest zeal to establish the
reign of what is called pure reason or nature, Christ
who is our sole Lord and Saviour having been excluded
from the minds of men and from the life and manners
of peoples[11].

In correlation with Christian metaphysics, in which
the human soul, the human reason, is created, Catholic
theology maintains that the Creator is free to propose to
man a teaching and revelation which are properly supernatural. Creation, by which man has access to the knowledge of God, is not the measure of all that man can know
of God. God can, besides, reveal to man what he deems
proper. The Vatican Council rejects the idea of a "sufficiency" of the reason, closed in upon itself. It is this sufficiency which the writers of the Council call rationalism.
One can add here that in fact this sufficiency is not reasonable.

Since man depends entirely on God as his Creator
and Lord, and since created reason is wholly subordi-
nate to uncreated truth, we are bound to give by faith
to God, when he reveals, the full submission of our
intellect and our will[12].

11 *Denz*, 1781.
12 *Denz*, 1789.

To this third Chapter of the Constitution *De Fide* is attached the canon which rejects the contrary doctrine:

> If anyone says that the human reason is to such a degree independent that faith cannot be commanded for it by God, let him be anathema[13].

The Church considers then that there are two sources of knowledge, the creation (experience), and revelation. Here Christian thought is opposed to the "rationalism" which allows only one source of knowledge—natural experience.

> The uninterrupted consensus of the Catholic Church held and holds that there are two orders of knowledge, distinct not only in principle but also in object; in principle, because in the one we know by natural reason, in the other by divine faith; in object because, over and above those things to which the natural reason can attain, there are proposed for our belief mysteries hidden in God which cannot be known unless divinely revealed[14].

In summation, Catholic theology has been determined to maintain, first, the power of the human reason, its dignity and capacity for metaphysical knowledge, against the Fideists and the Traditionalists; and second, the freedom of God to manifest himself, the possibility of the supernatural

13 *Denz*, 1810.
14 *Denz*, 1795.

and of revelation, against those who denied this possibility. Christian thought has traced its own path between the doctrines according to which human reason by constitution is nothing, or is radically disabled in consequence of original sin, and the metaphysics according to which human reason is the measure of the possible and the actual, and is ontologically independent and an absolute criterion. The human reason is created. It is not the absolute, or a particle consubstantial with the divine reason, but it is created *capax Dei*, capable of knowing God by creation and of knowing him by his word when it is spoken to man. One may then legitimately speak of a "Christian rationalism", if one means, as does modern science, a fundamental optimism about the power of the human reason, its rights, and its legitimate demands. But if one understood thereby that the human reason, in its present condition, would be the measure of all which exists or can exist, one would revert to making of the human reason an absolute criterion, or, even more simply, an absolute.

In this chapter concerning the doctrine of reason, a place may be assigned to the Catholic doctrine in which man—every man, even man outside the historical revelation—is capable of discerning the ethical requirements inscribed in objective reality, in him, in his conscience and, outside of him in nature, in virtue of the creation. This doctrine of the natural knowledge of the moral law is closely linked with the doctrine of the natural knowledge of God. In St. Paul, in the *Epistle to the Romans* (1:18 *et seq.*; 2:14), the two doctrines are taught side by side.

This doctrine is opposed to the thesis according to which

man only knows the will of God by supernatural revelation, and, with all the more reason, does not practise the moral law outside the people of God. The pagan virtues are thus vices.

Here again, Catholic theology and the theologies born of the Reformation diverge, following different principles. According to Catholic theology, the creation is a teaching of God, not only a teaching of his existence, of his divinity, and of his eternal power (*Romans* 1:18 *et seq.*), but also a teaching of his will. The creation bears the engraving of the principles which govern its existence and its completion. The natural law is that which allows and seeks completion of creation. Crime, or evil, is what destroys, annihilates, degrades, and reverses creation. Therefore, an objective principle of moral philosophy exists—the principle of completion, the very principle of creation. Pagans can discern this principle because their nature is not so damaged by original sin that they are incapable of discerning these ethical requirements which are inscribed in reality itself, and their freedom is not so affected that it is unable to choose the positive way. We see how this doctrine of the natural knowledge of the moral law is connected with the doctrine of human nature. According to several theologies born of the Reformation, man is incapable of discerning the ethical requirements inscribed in creation. Human reason is radically damaged by original sin, and man, outside the supernatural economy of the Church, is incapable of practising virtue because human freedom is abolished by the same original sin. We note then, on the plane of principles not only theological, but also philosophical, a marked divergence between the Catholic current and the Reformed current of Christian thought. Two, different, Christian philosophies had to be analyzed here. It is the doctrine or theory of original sin which appears at the center of, and as the key to, this separation between the two, Christian "branches". The theology born of the Reformation seems to have stressed some Augustinian tendencies which I have pointed out and which have been corrected by Thomism.

The doctrine of the natural law is finally set forth by St. Thomas Aquinas in the *Summa Theologica*, Ia IIae, *quaestio* 94. In article 4 of this question, St. Thomas asks whether the natural law is unique for all. He answers: "As regards the general principles of the reason, whether speculative or practical, truth is the same for all, and equally known. The natural law, as regards first principles, is the same for all". The pagans, before Christianity, outside Christianity, therefore can well discern the ethical principles derived from the natural law. The preaching of the Word to pagans is not a sowing of seed on ground lacking in any natural preparation, in any touchstone of anticipation. This touchstone which Paul sought, according to the book of the *Acts*, when he preached Christianity to the Athenians (*Acts* 17), made up of the *desiderium naturale sed inefficax videndi Deum*, "what therefore you worship, without knowing it, that I preach to you", and the possibility of a natural knowledge of God, is found here, on the ethical plane. The preaching of the Gospel encounters ground which is, to a certain extent that varies according to cases, pre-adapted to this preaching. The natural desire for justice, truth, fraternity, and authentic humanism forms the touchstone of anticipation, this natural pre-adaptation to the announcement of the supernatural message. And, on the other hand, even within the Christian economy, it is not only in virtue of a completely extrinsic law, dropped on man's head from the top of Mount Sinai, that man must respect man, but in virtue of a necessity immanent in his own conscience and in the very nature of creation. In contravening the moral law, man then does not only oppose a law supernaturally given to man by Moses; he sets himself at variance with his own will, his most deep-seated will, with his very being, with the very being of creation.

Therefore, it may be freely admitted that pagans (before or outside the Jewish and Christian economy, and men who today are placed outside Judaism and Christianity) perceive ethical requirements, sometimes more clearly and more profoundly than Jews and Christians, and avail themselves of them with, at times, more courage and more authentic human judgment than the children of the people of God. Jews and Christians may have to accept, from pagans or unbelievers, lessons in logic, humanism, and humanity, by virtue of this principle of a natural knowledge of moral exigencies.

One perceives—in Chapter IV of the Vatican Council already quoted, and in St. Thomas—that revelation sometimes bears relation to points which are accessible by the natural reason. Thus, the revelation of the Old Testament teaches us the existence of God, a creator, transcendant, distinct from the world, and it teaches us a natural, moral law, in the Decalogue. The existence of God and the moral law are, by right, the object of a knowledge possible for

reason without revelation. Revelation teaches us on the one
hand secrets which we would never have been able to discover by reason, because they surpass all that man could
hope for and imagine (for example, the promise of participation in the life of God), and on the other hand teaches us
truths which do not exceed, by right, the power of reason.
It tells us what reason is able to discover by its own powers.
Correlatively, one may say that in the Old Testament a
natural exercise of the human reason appears which, if one
may so put it, joins the Word of God. Thus, when the
Deutero-Isaiah bitingly censures fetishism and idolatry, he
expresses himself as a "free-thinker" and a "rationalist". He
makes use of his reason and applies himself to dispersing
the mythology which is at the foundation of idolatry. Revelation, or in this description, inspiration, does not then
come like a meteorite upon the inspired author; it does not
build upon him in a manner which is purely external, without the inspired author's co-operation in this inspired book.
The inspired author does not remain purely passive in the
process of inspiration. On the contrary, he exerts all his
faculties, and in particular his rational faculties. If one considers men like Amos, Jeremiah, Isaiah, and the anonymous
prophet whose oracles are combined with those of Isaiah,
one can say that inspiration prepared the ground, that God
pre-adapted for himself beings capable of hearing his word,
that he created at that time human personalities which were
remarkable from the intellectual and moral point of view.
Here, we have the meaning of the beginning of the *Book of
Jeremiah:* "Before I formed thee in the bowels of thy

mother, I knew thee; and before thou camest forth out of the womb, I sanctified thee".

Then, inspiration is not solely a process which goes from God to man; it presupposes in man a preparation, a pre-adaptation which is also the work of God and without which God could not speak the word to man. On man's part, a pre-adaptation is necessary in order that a co-operation may be possible. We meet again here, in connection with inspiration, ideas which were in connection with justification. Let me emphasize, once again, the profound homogeneity of Catholic theology in its different domains, its various compartments.

There is a margin, a substantial margin between what the reason can know by right of God and the natural law, and what it seems to attain in fact. So if it is by faith, according to the Vatican Council, that the human reason can have access to the knowledge of God by a reflection on the creation, it is a fact that the human reason has not attained to the conception of a unique, creative, transcendent, and free God, outside Israel. This fact is shown in the history of metaphysics and religion. A gap therefore exists between right and fact, between the possible and the actual.

In order to deal with this gap, we must advance some considerations regarding the relations which exist between freedom and intelligence. The human intelligence, in its exercise, has been affected, interfered with by man's sin. Paul points this out in the beginning of the *Epistle to the Romans*: "For the wrath of God is revealed from heaven

against all ungodliness and injustice of those men that de-
tain the truth of God in injustice, because that which is
known of God is manifest in them . . . When they knew
God, they have not glorified him as God, or given thanks;
but became vain in their thoughts, and their foolish heart
war darkened. . . ." (*Romans* 1:18 *et seq.*). It is an
established doctrine in the Old Testament that sin interferes
with, intervenes in the act of the intelligence. Stupidity,
according to the prophets, is a sin; it is *the* sin, the failure to
recognize God and his will. St. Thomas takes up the re-
frain, *stultitia est peccatum*[15].

At first sight, an apparent contradiction therefore exists
between this established doctrine according to which sin
becomes operative and intervenes in the act of the intelligence in order to diminish and indeed annihilate it, and the
doctrine according to which reasonable and free human
nature is not fundamentally damaged by original sin.

In fact, the established doctrine of Scripture, from the
Old Testament to St. Paul and St. John, maintains that
man is responsible for his intelligence. At the source of the
lack of intelligence there is a choice, a preference, which is
denounced by the author of the fourth Gospel: "They pre-
ferred the darkness to the light". But for this choice we are
all responsible. It is not our nature which imposes on us
this stupidity, this failure to recognize God and his will. It
is our freedom which is responsible. The doctrine which
Catholic theology rejects is that our nature would be to
such an extent damaged by original sin that our reason
would be incapable of attaining to the knowledge of God

15 *Summa Theologica*, IIa–II ae, q. XLVI, a. 2.

and our freedom would be annihilated. Catholic theology maintains that, by nature, we remain capable of knowing God, of discerning the ethical requirements which are written into the nature of things by virtue of creation, and of practising what is demanded by the natural law. But Catholic theology does not fail to recognize, on the contrary, that sin intervenes in the process of intelligence and in the discerning of first principles. What St. Paul, following the Old Testament, teaches is that human freedom can conceal from itself, by a process of "bad faith", truths which it has perceived. Human liberty can deflect, upset, damage, and falsify the intelligence. But this is not the result of human nature spoiled by original sin and transmitted in a depraved manner, since the first man; this is the work of man's present freedom. It is a process which renews itself every day. It is a question of present sin. A false mind is a mind which falsifies itself.

To place upon human nature the responsibility for a congenital lack of intelligence, for a radical failure to recognize God, and an absolute incapacity to discern the good and do it, is, *mutatis mutandis*, to adhere to a doctrine analogous to that of the Manicheans who held that man is a soul fallen into an evil world, into an evil body, and that in virtue of this evil principle, which is matter, evil is inevitable. It is not then, in this hypothesis, human freedom which is responsible, but the human condition, the blending of the divine soul with the evil nature of matter. Augustine and the whole Church have challenged this doctrine. Augustine and the whole orthodox tradition have maintained that

man is responsible for his own evil. To ascribe to a nature
damaged by original sin the responsibility for metaphysical
unintelligence and ethical blindness is still a way of evad-
ing the present responsibility for unintelligence and for the
servitude of freedom.

Conclusion

Conclusion

IN THESE RAPID SKETCHES I have only tried to demonstrate, for the sake of those who deny or doubt it, that an original Christian metaphysic does exist which is independent and autonomous, as opposed to other metaphysics recognized by history. Here, I have not attempted to justify this Christian metaphysic; I have tried simply to describe its broad outlines. The philosophical justification of Christian metaphysics requires another work, involving its own methods. The sole criterion, in order to justify this Christian metaphysic in the eyes of the philosopher, since revelation cannot be put forward, is objective reality itself, experience, which the reason knows. Then it is from objective reality, from experience, (which Christians call the created), that the human reason must proceed to this verification of the Christian metaphysic. We find ourselves faced with a number of metaphysics: the Brahminic, the Platonic, the Aristotelian, the Plotinian, the Spinozan, the Hegelian and others, and the Christian. A choice must be made, and the sole criterion at our disposal is reality, which is common to all. In the last resort, it is reality alone which is the judge. But this reality comprises certain aspects—

levels in which access is gained by different paths, by the positive sciences (physics, biology, psychology, and so forth), by metaphysical analyses, even by art, and by intuition. I do not have, here, to enter into this complex analysis of what reality can tell us from the metaphysical point of view.

In a word, we can now formulate our position with regard to the problem of Christian philosophy.

1. A metaphysical structure of Christian theology and dogma exists. Christianity comprises a metaphysical structure which is not any structure whatsoever, but which is, on the contrary, most original, in regard to what we learn from the history of metaphysical systems. I have tried to describe this metaphysical structure in its broad outlines, tried to point out its principal headings. It remains of course to supply the furniture, as it were, for these headings, to develop them, to bring forward documents which promise to be numerous. Christianity is thus not only a theology but also a metaphysic. Moreover, has the idea of a theology without metaphysical structure any meaning? I doubt it.

2. This metaphysical structure of Christianity is, fundamentally, the metaphysical structure of biblical theology. In other words, there is profound, substantial, structural continuity between the metaphysic inherent in biblical theology and the metaphysic of Christian orthodoxy. This is not surprising since the Christian authors, the Fathers, the Doctors, and the Councils constantly rely on Scripture in order to define what the Church thinks. In regard to the historians who asserted that Christianity, Catholic

Christianity at least, allowed Greek philosophy or the Greek philosophies to take the place of that which belonged to the biblical heritage, I maintain the opposite thesis. The thought of the Church, in its fundamental tradition, its Fathers, its Doctors, and its Councils, continues the thought of the Bible in everything that is essential. The outer covering of this thought may be Hellenic, Platonic, Aristotelian; at the fundamental level of structures and metaphysical theses, the Church has remained faithful to the biblical heritage. She has guarded the deposit.

3. Various Christian "shoots" or "branches" exist which mutually regard each other as heretical and unfaithful to the Scriptures. Here, we do not have to take sides. We have simply established that to a particular theology there corresponds a particular metaphysical substructure. That is true, even from the first centuries. One could, without doubt, reveal the metaphysical presuppositions of Arianism, Origenism, and Apollinarism. It is also true for the Great Schism of the West; the theologies of the Reformation do not have the same metaphysical principles as Catholic theology. It appears to me that, from the point of view of a description of underlying metaphysical structures, which is my point of view here, the *phylum* of Catholic theology continues the *phylum* of biblical thought in a substantially homogeneous way, both as regards the doctrine of creation and as regards the doctrine of human nature, freedom, and reason.

4. The exercise of philosophy is a purely rational exercise which must in no way depend on any supernatural revelation. Philosophy is autonomous, free, and mistress in

its own domain. The most jealous rationalism has nothing to fear from a concept of Christian metaphysics such as is presented by the foregoing considerations. The exercise of philosophy is an exercise of the reason which is based upon objective reality.

Catholic theology not only does not deny this, but allows it, and expressly asserts and encourages it. Human reason has its rights, its dignity, and its competence. The metaphysical theses which we have set forth in various chapters under the general title of "Christian metaphysics" are theses which are, by right, dependent upon pure reason and experience—with the exception of the doctrine of an entirely revealed supernatural calling, although in concrete experience one may discern, at least in depth, the traces of a call to this supernatural and gratuitous destination.

If the fundamental theses of Christian metaphysics have in fact been brought into a unity which is the biblical corpus, I would say that is not the fault of the Hebraic, Jewish, and Christian tradition; and there is nothing here which should jeopardize the rationality of these theses in the eyes of those rationalists who are most careful of preserving the autonomy of the reason. I may add, it is rather the fault of philosophies which have not been able to arrive at this rationality . . . If Aristotle and Plato taught that the heavenly bodies are divine and animated substances, and if Christianity, with Judaism, advanced the thesis according to which they are no such thing, it is not Christianity which must be taken to task, and the Christian doctrine on this subject is not compromised in its rationality because it is bound up with Christian theology. In truth, the heavenly bodies are not divine and animated substances. If Plato and Plotinus teach the eternal return, the substantial divinity of the soul and its fall into an evil body, transmigration, and yet other myths, we should not harbor resentment against Christianity for not having accepted them. In other words, if Christianity, with Judaism, has brought to the modern world rational, philosophic ideas, it is not Christianity which must be taken to task but the philosophies which, before it, did not bring forth these ideas.

These metaphysical theses which comprise and advance Christianity depend, by right, on pure reason, but they have only been understood, for the most part, within the People of God. Nothing is thereby lost to the rationality of these theses. They remain metaphysical theses. They remain verifiable by pure reason. But, historically, they proceed from the Jewish and Christian *phylum*. By right, no more is there a Christian philosophy than there is a Christian mathematics or a Christian physics. In fact, there is a Christian philosophy as there is a Euclidean geometry, a Riemannian geometry, a Newtonian physics, and an Einsteinian physics. In other words, the philosophy which we call Christian bears that name because of its historical origin.

Christian theology, for its part, will recognize, in this process of rationalization and demythologization which is at work in the whole of the Old Testament, in this new *phylum* which is the People of God, and in the Christian tradition after it, the work of the redemption, which regenerates the human reason which fails through the fault of men who kept truth captive in injustice and adored the created—heavenly bodies, natural forces, totems, and Caesars—instead of the invisible Creator, *baruk schemô*.

5. Between Christian theology and the metaphysic which is inwardly adapted and involved in it, organic relationships exist. Any theology is not compatible with any metaphysic. The autonomy of the properly philosophic order, which is grounded in objective reality, studied by the reason, is not diminished. Christian theology implies a metaphysical structure which is not any necessary structure whatsoever. If one touches on a certain metaphysical principle, the whole of Christian theology is aware of it. If, as seems to us, there is an adequate correlation between Christian metaphysics and objective reality, it is perhaps that a relationship exists which is neither one of opposition nor of disagreement between Christian theology and this same reality. The philosopher may be tempted by this thought to reflect upon the value of Christian theology. The theologian, for his part, knows that the author of nature is also he who spoke to Abraham, to Moses, and to the prophets, and at the end of time is revealed personally, without intermediary.

Index